Raising Children with Asperger's Syndrome and High-functioning Autism

by the same author

How To Be Yourself in a World That's Different
An Asperger Syndrome Study Guide for Adolescents
Yuko Yoshida, M.D.
Foreword by Lorna Wing
Translated by Esther Sanders
ISBN 978 1 84310 504 6
eISBN 978 1 84642 614 8

of related interest

Parenting a Child with Asperger Syndrome
200 Tips and Strategies
Brenda Boyd
ISBN 978 1 84310 137 6
eISBN 978 1 84642 420 5

The Complete Guide to Asperger's Syndrome
Tony Attwood
ISBN 978 1 84310 495 7 (hardback)
ISBN 978 1 84310 669 2 (paperback)
eISBN 978 1 84642 559 2

Key Learning Skills for Children with Autism Spectrum Disorders
A Blueprint for Life
Thomas L. Whitman and Nicole DeWitt
ISBN 978 1 84905 864 3
eISBN 978 0 85700 467 3

Aspergirls
Empowering Females with Asperger Syndrome
Rudy Simone
Foreword by Liane Holliday Willey
ISBN 978 1 84905 826 1
eISBN 978 0 85700 289 1

Raising Children with Asperger's Syndrome and High-functioning Autism
Championing the Individual

Yuko Yoshida, M.D.

Foreword by Lorna Wing
Translated by Esther Sanders and Cathy Hirano
Illustrated by Jun'ichi Sato

Jessica Kingsley *Publishers*
London and Philadelphia

Gillberg Diagnostic Criteria in Appendix 1 reproduced from Gillberg and Gillberg 1989 by permission of John Wiley and Sons.
Appendix 2 reproduced from *Kōkinō jiheishō, Asuperuga shōkōgun: "Sono ko rashisa" o ikasu ko sodate*, by Yuko Yoshida by permission of Chuohoki Publishing Co., Ltd.

This English language edition is published by arrangement with the Institute of Psychomedical Education for Children and Spectrum Publishing Company, Tokyo, Japan

First published in 2012
by Jessica Kingsley Publishers
116 Pentonville Road
London N1 9JB, UK
and
400 Market Street, Suite 400
Philadelphia, PA 19106, USA

www.jkp.com

Copyright © Institute of Psychomedical Education for Children 2009
English translation copyright © Esther Sanders and Cathy Hirano 2012
Foreword copyright © Lorna Wing 2012
Illustrations copyright © Jun'ichi Sato 2009, 2012

Library of Congress Cataloging in Publication Data
A CIP catalog record for this book is available from the Library of Congress

British Library Cataloguing in Publication Data
A CIP catalogue record for this book is available from the British Library

ISBN 978 1 84905 317 4
eISBN 978 0 85700 660 8

Printed and bound in Great Britain

Contents

Foreword

In this book, the author writes for parents of children with autism spectrum disorders, especially those whose children's level of ability is in the borderline, average, high or very high range, although much of what she writes is relevant for children with low or even very low ability. The book should also be read by professionals in the field, as it will deepen their understanding of the difficulties that parents have to deal with.

The first chapter explains the nature of autism in detail, but using clear, simple language. Throughout this book, the author's aim is to write in a way that parents of children with autistic conditions can understand and she succeeds brilliantly.

This chapter describes and analyses the nature of the problems that are fundamental to all forms of autism—namely the three basic problems affecting social behavior, known as "the triad." These are impairment of social interaction, social communication (verbal and nonverbal), and social imagination (that is, the ability to understand one's own thoughts and feelings, to be aware that other people have thoughts and feelings, and to be able to guess what those thoughts and feelings are in any particular situation). The author goes into considerable detail when discussing these problems, but always using the clear and simple language that is her special skill. She also describes the repetitive patterns of behavior closely associated with the triad and the other clinical features that can be seen, such as odd responses to sensory input. In addition, the author describes the other developmental disorders that can occur together with autism and the conditions that resemble autism. The author emphasizes the wide variations between individuals with autistic conditions.

Chapter 2 discusses how parents can use their knowledge of autism to help their child. She does this by analysing in great detail the problems experienced by children with autistic conditions, and discussing what parents can do to help. She, of course, emphasizes the importance of remaining patient while interacting with the child, and using methods of communication that are adapted to the child's level of ability. She points out how children with autistic conditions tend to have more problems with understanding communication than their expressive language would suggest.

Chapter 3 is called "The Way Forward." The first part concerns the need for parents to consult with medical, educational, and social specialists who understand autism (if such exist in the area where they live!). The author's own experience is that of services in Japan, but the types of services she discusses are to be found or are being developed in most English-speaking countries, and some other countries as well, so the advice is of value for English-speaking readers.

The second part of Chapter 3 describes the effects on siblings of having a brother or sister with autism and gives advice on how parents can reduce the adverse and promote the positive results of this experience. The author has a real and deep understanding of how difficult it is for parents to divide their time between a child with autism and their other children, who are not autistic, but may well have problems of their own.

In the last part of this chapter, the author looks at the feelings and needs of the parents. It is here that her empathy and profound understanding of the effects of autism on the parents and the whole family are shown most vividly.

As this is the foreword for the English version of Yuko Yoshida's book, it gives me great pleasure to write that the translators (Esther Sanders and Cathy Hirano) have produced a beautifully clear and simple, but detailed, translation that parents of children with autistic conditions will find enormously helpful and comforting. It is also very interesting to read the information in this book about Japan and the Japanese language and how parents in Japan cope with children with autistic conditions. It shows how similar are the problems faced by parents wherever they live. However, I shall always remember that dogs in Japan say "wan-wan," whereas those in England say "woof-woof"!

Lorna Wing
Consultant to the NAS Lorna Wing Centre for Autism

Introduction

Children with high-functioning autism (HFA) or Asperger's Syndrome (AS) are often misunderstood. They talk a lot, tend to march right up to people, and can argue like lawyers to get their way. They often do not get assistance in situations where they really need it, and instead they spend much of their childhoods being scolded and shunned. You, as a parent of such a child, are often misunderstood as well. You may be constantly criticized for not loving your child enough, for not providing appropriate discipline, or for being overprotective. This can cause you to lose confidence in your parenting ability and diminish your capacity to offer your child psychological support. The purpose of this book is to offer you medical information that will help make your efforts, and your children's efforts, more rewarding.

"What characteristics do children with HFA or AS have? What sort of things should I try doing at home as a first step? Who can I consult? How can I balance taking care of this child with raising my other children?" Parents at the clinic where I practice frequently ask these and other questions presented in Chapter 2. I have written this book to provide parents with concrete, easy-to-understand answers, explanations, and advice. I hope that those of you reading this book will find ideas that you will be inspired to try right now, today.

This book is primarily about children from infancy to early elementary school age with HFA or AS. It is with this age group that the true nature of these conditions, in terms of brain functioning, reveals itself most distinctly, unclouded by the effects of intellectual impairments (disabilities) or secondary disorders. However, the approach presented in this book can be applied to older children and to children who also have intellectual disabilities. Further, the ideas can be incorporated into strategies used by teachers in kindergartens, day care centres, elementary schools, and early intervention facilities who work with small groups of children.

The advice provided here represents only one of many practical approaches. Please keep this in mind and use the book in a way that best suits your family. I urge you to confront the problems before you precisely because you are concerned about them, rather than avoiding them out of fear or anxiety. That first step is sure to lead you to the solutions you need.

Introduction to the Revised Edition

Almost six years have passed since this book was first published in Japanese. By that time, a nationwide survey had already been conducted, in 2003, revealing that 6.3 percent of children enrolled in the regular public school system had some form of developmental disability such as high-functioning autism, attention deficit hyperactivity disorder (ADHD), or learning disability (LD). In 2005, the Act on Support for Persons with Developmental Disabilities clearly acknowledged the existence of developmental disabilities other than intellectual impairments. The importance of early detection of autism spectrum disorders (ASD) is now widely recognized, and, increasingly, various measures are being promoted as part of national policy. Understanding and support for people with high-functioning autism or Asperger's Syndrome is definitely advancing. At the same time, however, some parents who come to my clinic voice concerns like these:

> "Right now, we can still see him as being in the grey zone. But I'm constantly worrying that if we start doing something about his difficulties, it might turn the grey to black."

> "Ever since we were told that our child has autism, everything he does looks like a symptom. I find that so hard."

As a provider of support to young children, I think it is a tragedy when "early detection" actually makes parents and children feel cornered. The term "early detection" does not in fact fit the autism spectrum. In the case of diabetes or cancer, for example, early detection and early treatment mean finding an illness and nipping it in the bud before it becomes full-blown. Health exams to identify infants on the autism spectrum, however, are not aimed at nipping anything in the bud, but rather at identifying a certain brain type. This innate brain type is a personal characteristic that exists for life. Early identification, however, can help parents learn to sense their child's feelings of anxiety or tranquillity and to recognize his or her strong points and weak points. The infant health screening exams are a first step toward that.

Autistic characteristics are strengths. I hope that this book will help parents to believe that. This is what motivated me to write it in the first place, and that intent has not changed in this revised edition. All revisions are intended solely to convey my conviction more clearly. It is my sincere hope that you, as a parent, will be able to raise your child with pride and confidence and enjoy each day together.

Yuko Yoshida
May 2009

Chapter 1

What is Autism?

I. "Disability"— or "Individuality"?

Understanding the Characteristics of Development

Michitaka is four years old and his mother, Miyoko, is worried. "From the time he took his first step, Michitaka has never been what you could call settled. I don't remember ever having a leisurely walk together. I was always running after him. He started talking late, too. But, just as his grandmother assured me he would, he began remembering lots of words as soon as he turned three. 'Just like his father,' she told me.

"Once Michitaka started talking, he began approaching other children instead of spending all his time turning the water on or picking up stones, as he had until then. But although he has started playing with others, he still thinks that as long as he says, 'Can I have a turn?' it's OK for him to grab whatever they're playing with and take it away, no matter how many times I scold him. I'm always apologizing to the other mothers.

"He is much better at puzzles than other children, and he began reading at the age of two although I never taught him how. He must be a late-blooming genius. He has settled down gradually since he entered kindergarten, and I noticed he was following the teacher's instructions at the last parents' observation day. He's going to be fine. I worry too much. He talks great now, doesn't he? In fact he's almost too good at it. The other day on the train he started talking to the woman beside him. 'Hey lady! Do you know what my favorite train line is? The Hanzomon line! The purple stripe on the cars is so cool.' Honestly! I felt like butting in and saying, 'Don't you realize that strangers sitting beside you don't care what you like?' Even when someone answers his question, he never bothers to listen to what they say anyway. At least he could have said, 'Excuse me, Miss,' instead of 'Hey, lady.' He's going to wind up offending someone again! Is this really what you call having a gift for gab?

"But then again, he's really changed in this one year since he started kindergarten. Once he enters the five-year-old class, he'll be all right, won't he? It's all right to keep on like this just waiting to see how he does, isn't it? After all, the doctor never said anything was wrong at the three-year-old health screening, so he can't be autistic or have a learning disability, can he? Somebody please tell me. Somebody please say that everything's OK. Who should I ask? I can't ask anyone. I'm too afraid. But I don't think I can stand not knowing any longer. Somebody please help me!"

Michitaka's mother faces a very serious problem because she cannot find anyone who understands her situation. She has tried mentioning her concerns to other mothers in a light-hearted manner, but has been brushed off with such comments as, "You worry too much," or "But he can already write letters. How can you complain?" and even "Are you aiming to get him into a private school or something?" As her husband's response was only, "He's a good boy. I'll help you as much as I can, so hang in there," Michitaka's mother feels she cannot turn to him or to her mother-in-law for support.

Agonizing over Whether or Not to Consult Someone

When parents feel concerned about their child's development, the first thing they worry about is whether or not they really should be worrying: "Maybe I'm fretting over something that is just a matter of normal individual difference." "Maybe I'm just not a good parent." "Perhaps the children around here just happen to be unusually early developers. After all, most of them are girls." "I'm afraid to consult anyone about my worries because it might make them real."

Debating whether or not you should consult someone is distressing. No matter how hard you ponder this question, you are likely to go around in circles without getting anywhere. You may feel there is no one who can understand your anxiety. But any question or concern related to your child's development is worth consulting someone about. Consulting a professional can help ease the stress and confusion. Moreover, expert advice can often help you make beneficial changes in how you assist your child's development.

Professional Advice Can Help in Childrearing

Of 2,922 eighteen-month-old infants who received public health checkups in 2006 at a public health and welfare centre in Yokohama City, 667 (22.8%) were evaluated as needing some form of intervention. Of these, 572 (19.6%) were identified as requiring further observation for developmental problems (including behavioral problems such as hyperactivity). Results obtained from a checkup on 1,064 eighteen-month-old infants at another public health and welfare centre indicated that 203 (19.1%) required further observation for possible developmental disorders. In other words, one in five children who are eighteen months old may have problems. I can just hear some people saying, "It can't possibly be that many!"

A Swedish group, however, has reported similar figures. Gillberg and others at the Department of Child and Adolescent Psychiatry at Gothenburg University administered a health screening to 589 six-year-olds in their local area and designated certain children for further testing. They identified 63 children (10.7%) with neurodevelopmental or neuropsychiatric disorders (Landgren *et al.* 1996). The researchers then went back and examined some of the children who had passed the initial screening and found that some of these also had similar disorders.[1] Taking the proportion of the latter into consideration, they estimated the percentage of all six-year-olds with some form of neurodevelopmental or neuro-psychiatric disorder to be 21.8 percent, which is close to the figures of roughly 20 percent cited above.

We cannot blithely assume that this 20 percent is identical in meaning to that for Japan. The Japanese studies were conducted on eighteen-month-olds and the Swedish survey on six-year-olds, and the content of the examinations differed as well. These reports do suggest, however, that many children stand to benefit from childrearing practices that incorporate knowledge of developmental differences.

The Special Importance of Professional Advice in Cases of Subtle Impairment

I can now hear some people saying, "Well, if as many as one in five children have problems, there's nothing to worry about, right?" or "Aren't these cases just part of the usual range of individual differences?" The majority of these children fall within what is known as the "grey zone" of child development—a term that I frankly consider to be both inappropriate and offensive. In an argument that is only possible precisely because Japan has one of the best infant and child health checkup systems in the world,[2] some

---

1   Not all public health and welfare centres in Yokohama list the reason for classifying babies as "requiring further observation." The statistics quoted are from the two centres that do provide such figures.

2   Japan implements nationwide public health screenings that include testing for mental development. Ninety-three percent of eighteen-month-olds and 90 percent of three-year-olds undergo these checkups (Ministry of Health, Labour and Welfare 2007).

make the criticism that identifying and singling out children who fall within the "grey zone" actually fans parental anxiety. They go so far as to assert that, rather than trying to formulate an accurate profile of a child's development at regular checkups, physicians should focus on reassuring worried mothers and avoid detailed explanations even when parents express concern.

Gillberg and his colleagues, however, emphasize the importance of screening children and providing necessary support. They cite survey results indicating that children with unusual developmental characteristics tend to show better social adjustment at ages ten and eleven when their parents have early knowledge of these attributes (Gillberg *et al.* 1993). Similarly, research in Japan indicates that minor developmental disorders that are not targeted for continued support in infant and child checkups can hinder children's ability to succeed or fit in at school and can lead to their becoming socially withdrawn in adolescence or early adulthood (Kondo *et al.* 2002; Kurita 1991; Sugiyama 2001; Tanaka 2001).

If it is a common problem, does that mean there is no need to worry about it or that it is better not to concern yourself? Should you worry only if it is a "disability" but just wait and see if it is just a matter of "individuality"? Differences in understanding of this fundamental issue will cause differences in one's perspective on infant and child checkups. Let me first clarify my thinking on this issue.

"Disability" versus "Individuality"

So how do we distinguish between disability and the kind of individuality that could be called idiosyncratic, but normal in clinical terms? The generally accepted viewpoint is that serious symptoms constitute a disability, while only slight symptoms constitute merely

a normal variation. Not being able to walk by age five is a motor disorder, but always coming in last in races just means that the individual does not have a knack for athletics. Likewise, behavior that is so impulsive and careless it disrupts the classroom represents a disability, whereas being scatterbrained is just a personality trait. But is this perspective really helpful for the child?

Let me tell you a little more about Michitaka, the imaginary four-year-old introduced earlier. Michitaka will spontaneously talk about many different things in a very precocious way, yet he often cannot answer questions correctly. Take a look at one response he gave during an intelligence test:

Doctor: "Please finish the sentence for me. Your father is a man. Your mother is…?"

Michitaka: "My mother is a Miyoko."

Doctor: "Let's try again. Please finish the sentence. Your father is a man. Your mother is…?"

Michitaka: "… My mother is over there. See? Today she's wearing a skirt… I came with my mother by train today. We came on the Denen-toshi line. It has a purple stripe. When it gets to Shibuya it becomes the Hanzomon line because they share the same tracks. The train goes as far as Suitengu-mae, but sometimes the last stop is at Mitsukoshi-mae. What train line do you like? I like the Hanzomon line. I'm a boy so I like the purple stripe. You're a woman so why don't you pick the Asakusa line because it has a pink stripe? The Asakusa line shares tracks with the Keihin-kyuko line from Sengakuji."

Oh dear, now there's no stopping him. At first he was searching for the answer, feeling anxious, but now he's in full train mode. His mother heaves a sigh, thinking, "But I'm sure he knows the right answer to that question."

Watching Michitaka, the clinician thinks, "Perhaps he doesn't know the difference between 'man' and 'woman.' No, that can't be because he used those words himself. So maybe he didn't understand the meaning of the question. Oh, but he did 'finish the sentence' just as he was instructed to do. So that means he didn't realize that the first sentence was a clue. Other children would pick up on this immediately without being fazed. I'll have to examine his comprehension ability a little more thoroughly." In this way, the professional will analyse why Michitaka missed the point and formulate a plan for further assessment and the introduction of supports.

When a doctor or other expert thinks about Michitaka's behavior in this fashion, he or she is seeing it as the result of a "disability" (literally, a problem with his ability). But many professionals will very likely be having thoughts like these first: "'My mother is over there,' Ah, so that's where he's coming from. He caught me by surprise," "Even though he didn't understand, he still tried to think up an answer for me. Thank you!" "What a charming child," "He's very serious," "I bet the teachers at kindergarten are always scolding him for sidestepping their questions." The expert will smile inside at the boy's uniqueness and, at the same time, be touched by his sincerity or deeply moved by his childish innocence as he pours his heart and soul into efforts that will never be rewarded. At that moment in time, the professional is contemplating the child's behavior as a product of his individuality.

As professionals, we do not evaluate people in order to label them. We recognize when a child's lack of success is due to some weakness in ability and not to insufficient effort. We then think of a method that will make it easier for the child to obtain results. We fully appreciate the fact that he or she is struggling and striving in ways that other children are not, and we feel the same joy at the greatness of the results achieved. This is total acceptance of the child. It requires us first to accurately acknowledge the child's disability as a disability.

For example, no matter how hard a five-year-old who suffers from dyspraxia (a developmental coordination disorder) tries, he will spill food whenever he eats. Despite the fact that the child is trying very hard to do it right, a mother who is not aware that he has a disability may scold him, saying, "How many times do I have to tell you? Do you think you'll be able to go to elementary school if you keep doing that?" He will naturally feel sad and angry. And in order to protect himself from further hurt, he may criticize his mother, making such spiteful retorts as, "First grade still comes after kindergarten, whether I spill my food or not," or even "Shut up, you old witch!" Some children may resort to yet more drastic behavior. If their efforts continue to be negated, they will grow up to have a low self-image and no longer make any effort, saying, "What's the point in trying? I'll never succeed" and "I'm no good anyway." When the disorder is related to mental development in areas such as language, socialization, or flexibility, this trend will be even more pronounced. If we turn our eyes away from a disability and act as though it does not exist, we risk driving children into a corner where they lose their self-esteem.

I suggest that we refrain from seeing the concepts of "disability" and "individuality" as being diametrically opposed, or even mutually exclusive. No matter the child, any problematic characteristic is both a "disability" and a part of the child's "individuality." When you evaluate your child objectively and give him or her appropriate tasks or support, you are recognizing that characteristic as a "disability." When you view his or her heart-warming behavior with tenderness or are intrigued by his or her uniqueness, you are experiencing that child's special character (individuality), which he or she will retain for a lifetime. "Disability" and "individuality": these concepts only express the perspective from which you are viewing your child at a particular moment. And both are essential. I think that we must raise children with a balance of both these perspectives in order to enjoy childrearing and to support our children as whole human beings.

Viewing Autism as a Type of Unbalanced Development

What do you think of when you hear the word "development"? Physical growth, in which a child grows taller and gains weight, gradually reaching maturity? Intellectual growth, such as learning to speak and read and, later, embarking on the study of complex subjects?

In general, the expression "delayed mental development" refers to an overall delay in the acquisition of the type of intelligence measured by intelligence tests—in other words, IQ. In fact, however, the word development is often used more broadly. All abilities that we are not born with but that appear by adulthood are, by definition, areas of development. For example, the skills of adjusting one's behavior to the expectations of others, enjoying and cultivating a deepening of communication with others, and handling situations flexibly are all closely related to intelligence, yet

intellect alone does not guarantee their emergence. Each of these abilities belongs to an area of development distinct from that of the intellect. Normally developing children acquire these abilities to a degree commensurate with their level of intelligence. Development in some children, on the other hand, is unbalanced, and these skills remain conspicuously weak in comparison with their IQs. This is autism.

Autism is Not a Mental Illness

The word "autism" has traditionally been mistaken to mean an illness that causes people to close their minds and hearts to others and become withdrawn, and this gross misunderstanding still occurs even today. But the fact is, autism is not a mental illness. Nor is it the result of our failure as parents or of an unsuitable environment. It is a form of unbalanced development that is caused by certain characteristics of a child's brain. Medically, it is classified as a form of developmental disorder.

There are many different types of autism. In some children, the condition is accompanied by severe intellectual impairments that prevent speech, while in other children intelligence is intact. Children in the latter category do not fit the commonly held image of developmental disability and are therefore likely to be misunderstood as unloved, undisciplined, selfish, or mean. What they in fact need, however, are special educational supports to ameliorate the difficulties caused by their impaired ability.

The Wing Triad as a Basis for Diagnosing Autism

A diagnosis of autism is made when the level of development in three areas is lower than the level of intellectual development

(Wing 1998). English child psychiatrist and physician Lorna Wing identified those areas as follows:

1. Impairments of social interaction (the ability to interact with others and behave appropriately).

2. Qualitative impairments of communication (the ability to enjoy and cultivate deepening reciprocal interaction with others).

3. Qualitative impairments of social imagination (the ability to understand intuitively what cannot be seen or touched, such as how something came about, what might result, or relationships between things and concepts).

These criteria, first proposed by Wing, are often collectively referred to as the "triad of impairments," or the "Wing triad."

Why should children exhibiting this set of impairments uniformly be given a single diagnostic label? There are many reasons, one being that all children with the Wing triad develop according to the same set of principles. In other words, determining whether a child is autistic or not according to these criteria is equivalent to selecting a set of principles that can be used in deciding what and how to teach that child in order to provide the most effective help.

Because even children diagnosed as autistic will manifest their impairments in different ways, determining through observation of behavior whether or not the triad is present is difficult and requires skill. Even the behavior of the same child will change according to age and stage of development. The second section of this chapter ("The Autism Spectrum") gives specific examples of what the Wing triad looks like during the preschool to early elementary school years.

High-functioning Autism and Asperger's Syndrome

The Wing triad is manifested in many different ways. A child may at first glance appear to be very friendly and talkative. He may appear to lack any idiosyncratic behaviors such as insisting on lining objects up in a row. But if you look closely, you will notice that he lacks social common sense, has a hard time realizing when he has hurt someone's feelings, and tends to miss the point in conversations. He is governed by rules, which he adheres to inflexibly. When the triad appears in this form it is called Asperger's Syndrome. In other words, Asperger's Syndrome is a subtle, atypical form of autism that, on the surface, does not appear to be autism. The difference between high-functioning autism and AS is in how the triad is manifested (see the figure on page 28).

High-functioning autism, on the other hand, is defined merely as autism that is not accompanied by a clear delay in intellectual development, and the word "high-functioning," in fact, refers specifically to IQ—usually defined by a score of 70 or above (represented by the upper half of the oval on the left hand side of the figure). In this case, the manifestation of the triad does not follow the distinctive pattern seen in AS, and the autistic symptoms are often much more pronounced. While the definition of AS is not IQ based, the distinctive pattern in which the triad of impairments manifests itself means that most people with AS are not intellectually impaired.

The definitions and distinctions presented here are in accordance with those of Lorna Wing. They differ slightly from the classifications and diagnostic criteria set forth by the American Psychiatric Association (publisher of the DSM-IV manual; APA 1994) and from those of the World Health Organization (publisher of the ICD-10 manual; WHO 1992).

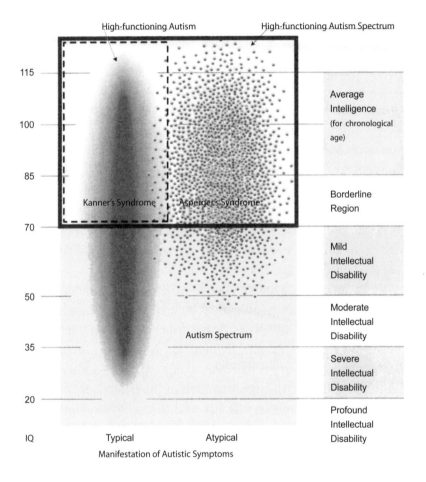

**High-functioning Autism and Asperger's Syndrome
(Wing's Approach)**

Asperger's Syndrome and Autism: Defining the Autism Spectrum

Wing also proposed use of the term "autism spectrum" to express a concept that includes both autism and Asperger's Syndrome. Like the yellow and red stripes in a rainbow that are simply different wavelengths of light, autism (also known as Kanner's autism or Kanner's Syndrome) and Asperger's Syndrome (or Asperger Syndrome) are part of the same continuum, even though they appear to be totally different. Wing emphasizes that the choice of treatment depends primarily on whether or not the triad of impairments is present (i.e., whether or not the individual is on the autism spectrum) and that there is not much point in trying to distinguish between Kanner's Syndrome and Asperger's Syndrome. Although in the previous figure I have clearly differentiated the autism spectrum (the large grey box) and, within that, Kanner's Syndrome and Asperger's Syndrome, there is in fact no precisely defined point of demarcation in terms of symptom severity or type.

The Meaning of High-functioning

Although the term "high-functioning" conveys an image of someone who is socially well adjusted, this is inaccurate. All the word really means is that the individual does not exhibit any clear delay in intellectual development on intelligence tests (i.e., that he or she has an IQ of about 70 or more). In the previous figure, the box encompassing IQs of 70 or more represents the high-functioning autistic spectrum. Moreover, owing to variations among the different tests used to measure IQ, the standards for determining delayed intelligence are not strictly uniform. Thus, the phrase "no clear delay in intellectual development" includes people with higher than average intelligence, people with average intelligence, and people in the borderline region. Even children without autism spectrum disorders will have a hard time keeping up in a mainstream class of forty[3] or so children if their intelligence is on the borderline (about 70 to 85). Children who have autism spectrum disorders and only borderline intelligence will find it even harder. In other words, "high-functioning" does not necessarily mean that the individual will be able to function in a mainstream classroom.

Better Quality of Life is More Important than IQ

In early childhood it can be difficult to judge whether a child is high functioning or not. Sometimes the IQ of children with a mild intellectual disability (an IQ of about 50 to 70), and very occasionally of children with a moderate intellectual disability (about 35 to 50), will increase to borderline levels (about 70 to 85) or even higher as they grow older.

When I mention this fact, parents and teachers often ask me how to increase a child's IQ or wonder if these occurrences are the result of specialized interventions. Professionals treating children with autism spectrum disorders, however, do not view increasing IQ scores as a goal of intervention; even if it were theoretically possible to raise these test scores in isolation as a direct result of treatment, this would not improve children's quality of life. There are many individuals whose verbal IQ scores are inflated by an ability to memorize dictionary definitions, while in everyday life they are utterly unable to carry on a proper conversation. There are also children whose IQ scores increase without any specialized intervention. In such cases, the children's brains appear to be

---

3   The maximum class size in Japan is forty students.

following a pre-programmed process of development. Where IQ is concerned, the best that can be said for any appropriate intervention strategy is that it will not interfere with this natural process.

Moreover, I firmly believe that what can be achieved through intervention is actually of far greater value than higher intelligence on paper. I say this having examined numerous adults with high IQs who have Asperger's Syndrome but were not diagnosed (and therefore not treated) during childhood. So many of them suffer from poor self-image and feelings of rejection, relationships with their parents that are damaged almost beyond repair, and the need to resign themselves to a level of accomplishment beneath their potential in terms of raw ability. A child's sense of self-worth cannot be achieved by raising intelligence test scores, a fact we must take to heart.

When you Hear "PDD," Think "ASD"

Your child may be diagnosed as having pervasive developmental disorder (PDD) or pervasive developmental disorder not otherwise specified (PDD-NOS). These terms are explained in Appendix 1. If your child has been diagnosed with one of these conditions, the way forward for you and your child will be just as clear—or even clearer—if you mentally replace the PDD label with the term "autism spectrum disorder." It is important not to misunderstand and think, "It's PDD, so my child is not autistic," or "It's PDD-NOS, so treatments for autism are not relevant." PDD means "autism and related disorders." Therefore, while the name PDD-NOS may sound to you like a whole different kettle of fish, children with this diagnosis will respond well to supports that are based on the premise of the triad of impairments.

The same can sometimes be said of learning disabilities, as some physicians lump the features of the triad of impairments under the designation "LD." (In particular, if you are told that your child has a "nonverbal LD," you can in most cases assume that this is just another name for an autism spectrum disorder.) For more on this subject, please see page 101.

II. The Autism Spectrum

The following outline may help consolidate your understanding of the autism spectrum:

1. The Wing triad as a set of diagnostic criteria
★ Impaired socialization and qualitative impairment in social interaction
★ Qualitative impairments of communication
    * Difficulty with expressive language
    * Difficulty with receptive language
    * Difficulty with nonverbal communication
★ Qualitative impairment of social imagination
2. Symptoms outside of the Wing triad

These disabilities take many different forms, depending on the individual. In this section, I will explain the forms they most commonly take in preschool children and early elementary school children on the high-functioning end of the autism spectrum. The examples given here are not necessarily all present in every affected child. Moreover, the symptoms exhibited even by the same child will change as he or she grows. Skill is needed to discern the developmental causes that underlie behavior in any given case.

1. The Wing Triad as a Set of Diagnostic Criteria
Impaired Socialization and Qualitative Impairment in Social Interaction

If asked to describe the images they tend to associate with the words "autism spectrum," many people will mention, for example, having an aversion to human interaction or a tendency to "hide inside a shell." In fact, however, the medical diagnosis is not based solely on quantitative measures of the amount of interaction with others.

When we talk about qualitative impairment of interactions with others, we are referring to behavior that cannot be explained simply as social immaturity of the kind seen in cases of intellectual disability. Let's take Michitaka. He will talk to strangers about his favorite subject, trains, and be oblivious to the other person's reaction, whether it is surprise or anger. In contrast, around the time that typically developing children begin speaking, they also begin to display the ability to distinguish between family and non-family members and between situations in which it is acceptable to talk to someone and those in which it is not. This is why children who follow a typical pattern of development, regardless of their age, will not ordinarily talk to strangers. To the extent that Michitaka frequently does so, his behavior cannot be classified as appropriate for any age range and he would be assessed as having a qualitative impairment of social interaction.

Similarly, when a child with the IQ of a three-year-old still engages primarily in parallel play of the kind usually seen in children of around age two (i.e., playing side by side without interacting), the child's social development is not commensurate with his or her intellectual level. Few children with ASDs, however, exhibit only uneven development of ability. Careful observation reveals that from an early stage they also display unusual traits not seen in neurotypical youngsters. In addition, atypical characteristics that were not obvious at an early chronological age, or at a low developmental age, often become evident as these children mature.

The difficulty children with ASDs have sharing the same behaviors, feelings and common sense as others in their everyday social circle can also be considered an impairment in the development of social interaction.

One-sided Interaction with Others

Interaction between people involves a constant back-and-forth exchange of feelings and actions. When you do or say something vis-à-vis another person, you then gauge his or her reaction, and what you feel, say, or do next is a response to that reaction. This is reciprocity. Reciprocal relationships are always evolving in the sense that the interaction moves forward in a way that depends on what each party says or does.

Children with ASD, even those who appear on the surface to be interacting, find it difficult to attain true reciprocity. They say what they want to, when they want to, and then go their merry way. When playing "house," for example, they may behave like movie directors using other children as actors in their own predetermined script. Even actions that superficially appear to be the essence of kindness and thoughtfulness are sometimes simply one-sided sequences of behavior, for instance dictating actions to a passive, compliant child or performing the ritual—always and without exception—of patting a crying child on the head and saying, "There, there." Depending on the other person and on the circumstances, such actions may at times be highly appreciated but at other times may be confusing or off-putting. Children with ASD, however, tend to remain unaware of other people's expectations for appropriate behavior in a given situation; therefore, they often repeat these inappropriate behavior patterns from one encounter to the next. When interacting with grownups, this type of one-sided behavior may remain undetected, as adults have a natural tendency to adjust their own behavior to match the tempo of the children they're with. Children with autism spectrum disorders often prefer to interact with adults who respond in a predictable way.

Lack of Reciprocity in Peer Friendships

Interaction with peers gives the clearest indication of the quality of social skills. Children with autism spectrum disorders generally find it very difficult to build reciprocal relationships with age mates. Of course, many simply have no interest in friendships, but even those who are interested often prefer to play with children who are either older or younger: they depend on the former to take their abilities into consideration or give them clear instructions on how to behave, and on the latter to do as they are told. Their relationships with same-age children are often limited to sharing the same equipment, such as swings or sandboxes, and toys such as video games, or to a specific type of interaction with a specific child, such as one-sided bossing or being bossed. Such peer relationships are neither reciprocal nor evolving. If, however, such behavior does not result in any obvious problems during early childhood, teachers at kindergartens and day care centres are unlikely to raise any red flags. Frequently the problem becomes apparent only after the child has entered elementary school, particularly from around the age of nine or ten, but tracing his or her developmental history reveals that it actually began much earlier.

Inability to Act Appropriately in a Given Situation

The ability to act appropriately may sound highly sophisticated, but in fact there is such a thing as "age appropriateness" even with respect to two-year-olds. When adults are very subdued, such as at a funeral, typically small children will appear anxious and uncomfortable. Some may cry but very rarely will a child laugh out loud. They monitor the behavior of their parents or other adults, trying to determine how they should act.

Children with ASDs, however, find it extremely difficult to read the atmosphere or nonverbal cues. If they see something funny, they will laugh without restraint and if they feel like singing, they will burst into song. As their awareness of how others perceive them is very low, they continue their behavior and will tend to repeat it on similar occasions.

Lack of Age-appropriate "Common Sense"

"Common sense" refers to social rules that are picked up without explicit instruction and that come naturally to everyone in that culture or community. Invisible social boundaries are an example. Children with neurotypical development will not enter another person's house without being invited. They do not need to have it explained that trespassing is a crime; they just naturally hesitate to invade another person's "territory." Similarly, they will not go behind the counter or enter the kitchen in a restaurant. The same is true concerning physical distance from other people. Without being taught, two- or three-year-old children know who it is OK to touch and who not, and by the time they reach elementary school they are able to adjust the distance between themselves and their conversation partner according to the degree of familiarity in their relationship. It is not unusual for children on the autism spectrum, however, to need a sort of "how-to" guide, with each of these rules regarding social boundaries taught explicitly, one by one.

Their sense of modesty also tends to be insufficient. They may know the word "embarrassed," but most often do not really have the concept, as becomes clear when a first-grader with an ASD unperturbedly changes clothes in front of someone of the opposite sex or walks out of the washroom with his or her pants still partly down. At the same time, some will squirm with embarrassment for no discernible reason.

To take another example, typically developing children seem to acquire a respect for life without any explicit education. A toddler may pull the legs off an insect without feeling any qualms, but at some point most children begin to feel aversion to killing other living things or recognize naturally that a pet or human being, even when dead, is not a mere object. Some children with ASDs have difficulty acquiring this sensibility. One boy, for example, threw his dead pet into the wastebasket in his bedroom without giving it a thought. When scolded by his mother, he apologized as follows: "I'm sorry. I should have put it in the compost instead of the bedroom wastebasket." Another child straddled the corpse of her grandmother when it was laid out for burial. In both cases, the children genuinely did not have the common sense to know that their behavior was inappropriate and to realize the feelings such actions would inevitably arouse in the people around them.

Inability to Recognize or Conceptualize One's Own Feelings

Children with ASDs have difficulty expressing their emotions in ways that others can easily understand. They may grin when troubled or look sulky when they are not angry at all. Not only do they have difficulty expressing emotions, it seems that they also have trouble recognizing (even within their own minds) what their feelings are and conceptualizing or expressing them in words.

In adult psychiatry there is a condition called alexithymia. Patients are unable to recognize their own feelings and instead exhibit emotions in the form of psychosomatic illnesses. For example, a person under severe stress because he has been transferred to a new department at work may only realize the extent of his psychological fatigue after he has collapsed from a gastric ulcer. Similarly, many people on the autism spectrum work to breaking point because they are unable to say, "I need a rest." Then, one day they are suddenly no longer able to go to school or work. Rather than being caused by a communication impairment that prevents them from speaking up, the condition appears to be similar to alexithymia. They simply find it difficult to recognize that they are extremely tired or overwhelmed. Sometimes I see people with ASDs who appear to be so anxious their mouths have gone dry. And yet when asked, "Are you nervous?" some will flatly deny it. They are aware of their mouths being parched, but by way of explanation may simply say, "Sometimes I get like that." They have difficulty conceptualizing their conditions with words such as "nervous." Temple Grandin has Asperger's Syndrome yet runs her own business and is also a university professor. She once explained that she does not understand the meaning of the word "happy." When someone uses this word, she translates it into the feeling she experiences when eating French toast with lots of honey on a Sunday morning. Difficulty conceptualizing emotions is a symptom of both impaired socialization and impaired social imagination, which is addressed later.

Judging from reports on adult cases, it can be supposed that the same difficulty in recognizing one's own feelings also occurs during childhood. The whirlpool of such emotions as anxiety and frustration must be a source of distress that is all the more profound in individuals who lack the ability to understand what they are experiencing. It is no wonder that this can lead to meltdowns.

Emotional Separateness: Feelings that Others Find Difficult to Share

Although it is clear that children with ASDs experience a wide range of emotions, it is often difficult for other people to share them. For example, we may wonder why a child seems so happy looking at a road sign, or why he or she is so frightened by a man with a beard. Although we can explain it by saying, "He (she) is always like that" and be happy or sad on the child's behalf, we may find it impossible to empathize. Children with Kanner's Syndrome, for example, will sometimes laugh out loud for no apparent reason, while those with Asperger's Syndrome often grin to themselves. Presumably they have their reasons, but such "vacant" grins or laughter are emotional states in which those around them simply cannot partake.

Some children on the spectrum become frightened or cry in situations where others would not. Some are terrified of things that are not usually objects of fear, such as an emergency exit sign or a specific page in a picture book. Even if the object is something that typically developing children might tend to be afraid of, such as a dog, an insect, the dark, or thunder, the emotional intensity is excessive. When a child sobs because his neatly arranged row of Hot Wheels cars has been pushed out of alignment, others may comprehend his feelings intellectually, but they cannot actually experience or share the same emotion.

Emotional Separateness: Difficulty Sharing the Feelings of Others

It is also difficult for people with ASDs to be receptive to and to share the feelings of others. When he sees another child crying, a child on the spectrum may peer into the other's face with avid curiosity, offending both that child and his mother. When his beloved mother falls down the stairs and is curled up in pain, he may point his finger at her and laugh because the way she is sitting looks funny to him. Just because he behaves in this way, however, it does not mean that he is heartless or that he does not like the other person. This lack of sympathy is, rather, a fundamental symptom of his condition and another example of qualitative impairment in social interactions.

Common Behaviors in Early Childhood

How does this type of qualitative impairment appear in babies who are on the spectrum? Many reports describe a failure to actively demand the mother's attention—a toddler, for example, may not follow his mother everywhere as would usually be expected—or a tendency to demand her attention in ways that are odd. Toddlers with ASD may become excessively upset or anxious the moment the mother passes out of the line of vision as she is leaving home, but then forget all about her and play happily once she has disappeared. Similarly, they may show little interest when the mother returns home and continue to watch a favorite video for twenty or thirty minutes without once seeking her attention. Infants may rarely hold out their arms seeking to be picked up or fail to cling to the parent's body when held.

Many reports also identify a lack of stranger anxiety. The baby may wail loudly whenever Grandpa comes over, but then meet a female guest for the first time and be perfectly unperturbed; at root may be an extreme fear of men in general, or of people with specific characteristics such as a beard or glasses. Or stranger anxiety may be excessive and coupled by extreme attachment to the mother, to the extent that even at age one or two the child may refuse to be cared for by his father. Another variation on the theme of oddity is when maternal attachment and stranger anxiety first appear at the age of two or three.

Qualitative impairment of interaction with others is also exhibited by a lack of response when played with, or by an underdeveloped ability to imitate. Reports often cite difficulty getting very young children with ASDs to enjoy action songs. Many babies on the spectrum show no interest in action songs at all, but some will watch intently without participating and then perform the actions by themselves at another time. They have the ability to memorize but do not understand the fun of mimicking.

Lack of interest in other people is also a concern during early childhood. Most children with ASDs begin to show an interest in or to pay attention to adults by the time they are two or three, but one-way interaction is conspicuous. They may, for example, climb into another mother's lap without any hesitation, completely unconscious of invisible social boundaries, or grab the hand of anyone who happens to be nearby to ask for help getting something they want. This type of interaction is often described as "using people as tools." In addition, children on the spectrum sometimes

endlessly demand that their mothers play the same game with them in exactly the same way or that they answer the same questions over and over again. These behaviors are often mistaken as an indication of sociability or a budding interest in other people, but in fact they are simply routines or perseverations that involve other people. A child who "interacts" with his mother this way is basically using her as a walking, talking, life-sized doll.

Qualitative Impairments of Communication

Communication can be either verbal or nonverbal, both of which in turn can be either expressive (communication that involves conveying information) or receptive (communication that involves receiving information).

A great many parents seeking advice are concerned about verbal communication, and particularly about expressive language, but in ASDs qualitative impairments can occur in both verbal and nonverbal communication.

Difficulty with Expressive Language

Children with ASDs often show delayed speech development, while some begin speaking at the usual age. Many of the latter, however, exhibit certain biases in the type of vocabulary they acquire. When a child demonstrates verbal interaction that is either odd or very limited, or makes peculiar mistakes in expression, and these behaviors cannot be explained by delayed development—that is, they are out of proportion with the child's developmental age in terms of verbal skills—then we say that the child has a qualitative impairment of verbal communication.

TALKING TO ONESELF (MONOLOGUING)

Typically developing children learn words that they need in everyday life (Papa, Mama, and so on) and then try them out immediately, realizing that the whole point in acquiring words is to use them with other people. Children with autism spectrum disorders, too, can say the names of things they are interested in or words that they hear frequently. Often, however, they do not use words (such as Papa or Mama) for the purpose of calling to people and instead spend most of their time engaging in oral output that is not directed at anyone in particular (sometimes called "monologuing"). While all children monologue to some extent, this behavior is much more pronounced in those who are on the spectrum, and the content of their speech has distinctive characteristics. The monologues of children with ASDs often consist of delayed echolalia (discussed below), "live broadcasts" of running commentary on their thoughts and actions, and lines from a "play" in which they are the sole writer, actor, and director.

Many parents are highly distressed by these monologues, embarrassed to see their children behaving in a way that seems so flagrantly autistic and begging them not to do it in public. Often, however, this self-talk helps the child to endure anxiety or to make a transition from one emotional state to another. I suggest that parents observe the child closely to understand the circumstances in which monologuing tends to increase before considering how to deal with it.

JARGON

Some children on the spectrum join sounds together to make "words" that do not exist in any language and then use these invented words as if they have meaning. This is called jargoning.

Parents will sometimes say affectionately, for example, "Oh, there goes my son, speaking Michitaka-ese again!" Children may jargon either during monologues or when addressing other people; in the latter instances it may seem as though they are really attempting to make genuine conversation.

ECHOLALIA

The most well-known example of odd communication in children with ASDs is parroting. All children parrot when they are first learning language, but once they develop to the stage where they can confirm meaning by asking, this behavior naturally ceases. Children with ASDs, however, may continue parroting (engaging in echolalia) in certain situations even when they get older. The precise definition of the term "echolalia" varies from one expert to another; I am using it here in the broad sense of "repetition of words spoken by another person." There are two forms: immediate echolalia, in which the other person's words are repeated verbatim at the time they are heard, and delayed echolalia, in which words that were heard previously are repeated at a later time.

In some cases echolalia is simply mechanical repetition without any communicative function, while in other cases—depending on the child's level of development—it is meaningful. For example, immediate echolalia may be used to mean, "I don't understand what you've just said." Delayed echolalia can have a number of uses, including self-stimulatory monologues as a form of solo play; patterns that are repeated whenever the child is prompted by a specific situation, such as saying, "Red means stop" every time a traffic light is encountered; repetitions of words that help the child deal with his or her feelings; or expressions of anxiety or conflict. Another way in which delayed echolalia is used is as a means of conveying a specific message: when the child wants to stop doing something, for example, he or she might signify this by saying, "Goodbye, everybody!"—parroting the words his kindergarten teacher says at the end of every class.

In children with Asperger's Syndrome it is not uncommon for monologuing and echolalia to almost completely cease by the age of five or six. Some children with Asperger's Syndrome are also reported to have shown almost no signs of echolalia from early childhood.

DIFFICULTY WITH EXPRESSIONS INVOLVING PERSPECTIVE

As people with ASDs have a strong tendency to learn by memorizing patterns, they have a very difficult time learning to adjust their position vis-à-vis the listener. When they come home, for example, instead of saying, "I'm home!" they may say, "Welcome home!" since they often hear these words when entering the house. When asking for a chocolate, Ken, who has Kanner's Syndrome, says what the listener to such a request might say: "Here's a chocolate for Ken." These types of linguistic errors can be considered a form of meaningful delayed echolalia, because they are repetitions of language heard on a prior occasion and then applied to a similar situation—in this case, with the roles reversed. In English these errors are also known as "pronoun reversals": Ken, for example, might make his request by saying, "Ken, I'll give you a chocolate," when he means to ask, "Would you give me a chocolate?"

Not all children with Asperger's Syndrome make mistakes as obvious as those above, and those who do often outgrow these errors at an early age. On the other hand, it is not uncommon even for these children to continue to have difficulties with relational antonyms and similar word pairs (give/take, go/come, here/ there, and so on) all the way through the middle of elementary school.

UNIQUE COINAGES

Families with children who are on the autism spectrum may have their own special lexicon. For example, the child might use invented language, such as a nonsense word like "pamachi" to mean "I want to go for a drive" or "con-case-er" instead of "container." "Open it!" might be the child's catch-all expression when making a request of any kind, or he might say, "I want to go to Pocky," with this word being a stand-in for the Train and Bus Museum (located in a suburb of Tokyo) where his parents once bought him a package of Pocky-brand chocolate-coated pretzels. The words will make sense to the child's family, but not to outsiders.

PEDANTRY

When children on the autism spectrum reach school age, they begin to acquire more and more words from the conversations of adults and from books or the news, and some begin to use expressions, such as "so-called" or "environmental destruction," that seem conspicuously too advanced for their age. Or, they may go into long-winded detail or be excessively precise, to the point of eccentricity, in their use of numbers or words. Take, for example, this conversation between a parent and child.

> Parent: "We got these cookies from Grandma a few days ago, didn't we?"
>
> Child: "Not a few days ago. It was March 28th! Grandma bought them for us for 248 yen. And they aren't cookies; they're Marie-brand biscuits!"

Similarly, some children may be finicky in their pairing of certain nouns and verbs, insisting that every use of the word "problem" must be coupled with the word "solve" and correcting anyone they catch using the expression "do a problem."

Behavior of this type—excessive precision, the use of sophisticated vocabulary, and intense fascination with exact numbers or other details—is known as pedantry and is one feature commonly found in children with Asperger's Syndrome, particularly once they reach school age. Although there is a native Japanese word—*gengakuteki*—that is equivalent to the English word "pedantic," for the sake of clarity and specificity, Japanese professionals in the field of autism have adopted the transliteration of the English word "pedantry" as the preferred term for this concept.

ONOMATOPOEIA: TOO CLOSE TO THE REAL THING

In Japan the term *koro-koro* is used to express the movement of "rolling." This type of imitative word is referred to linguistically as "mimesis," and it should be fairly obvious that the use of mimesis varies widely from culture to culture. What is somewhat less obvious, however, is that words expressing sounds (linguists call this "onomatopoeia") also vary by culture and, as such, are examples of agreed-upon social convention. For example, when asked what a dog sounds like when it barks, most Japanese children will say, "Wan-wan!" whereas a child from England would most likely say, "Woof, woof!"

In contrast, some children with autism spectrum disorders make sophisticated, ultra-realistic imitations of animal cries or machine sounds. They can bark so much like a dog that the sound cannot be captured in letters, or distinguish between the noises made by the engines of different brands of automobile or between the sound

made by train doors when they open versus the sound made when they close. This ultra-realism, in place of what we usually think of as onomatopoeia, is probably related to the fact that children with ASDs have difficulty mastering the relevant cultural conventions. Some may also be particularly talented at processing sounds that intrigue them.

IMITATION AND REPETITION

Some children on the spectrum imitate wholesale the speech patterns of others, sometimes right down to tone of voice. They may always speak in unmistakable imitation of a particular and well-known cartoon character, for example, or adopt a more feminine or masculine tone depending on the gender of the homeroom teacher they happen to have that year. Some children will use popular television phrases—such as "final answer"—over and over, ad nauseam.

Even children who do not copy speech in this way will tend to continually bring up the same topics of conversation and ask the same questions again and again even when they already know the answers. This type of repetition is indicative of both a qualitative impairment in communication and an impairment of imagination.

LACK OF RECIPROCITY IN CONVERSATIONS

Some children with autism spectrum disorders are very talkative, like the imaginary four-year-old boy, Michitaka, introduced at the beginning of this book. One of the most noticeable symptoms that these youngsters display is a lack of reciprocity in their conversations. Children like Michitaka find it hard to shift their feelings in response to what other people say to them, and they tend to speak in a conspicuously one-sided manner and only about their own interests. They have learned to enjoy talking, but have not yet learned the value or enjoyment that can be obtained by tuning in to how others respond or listening to what they have to say. Preschool children on the spectrum exhibit a range of difficulty in this area: some are in general completely out of sync with their conversation partners, while others show no noticeable difficulty with reciprocity at all. Actually, however, evaluating this area of development in early childhood is difficult, since even typical preschoolers tend to be one-sided in making conversation. Children on the high-functioning end of the autism spectrum will often begin to show a pronounced lag in reciprocity from around the third or fourth grade of elementary school.

As seen with Michitaka, some children may ostensibly be asking a question, but in fact do not really care to have it answered and will either plough ahead with their own thoughts without waiting for a response or instruct the other person on what his or her answer should be. Lack of reciprocity in conversations is closely related to the ability to consider what is going on in the other person's mind, which brings us to a concept known as "theory of mind."

DIFFICULTY CONSIDERING WHAT OTHERS ARE THINKING

When children (and adults) with ASDs speak, they have trouble recognizing what the listener might be thinking or what he or she already knows about the topic and adjusting what they say accordingly. Consequently, they may suddenly begin talking from somewhere in the middle of a train of thought, as if they are continuing a conversation that has already begun; in addition, they may speak in a way that assumes the other person has prior knowledge of the topic, when in fact this is not the case. For example, when a child with an ASD goes to buy shoes, he may explain proudly to the sales clerk, "They're just like Takashi's" (while the clerk wonders, "Who in the world is Takashi?!") or, when asked for a riddle, may come up with, "What's my favorite food?"

Normally developing children generally acquire the ability to consider and make suppositions about the thoughts of others from around ages four to six. Consequently, problems in this area may not be spotted, even by a professional, during the preschool years. When a person is able to distinguish what is in another person's mind from what is in his own, we say that he has acquired a "theory of mind" (for more about which, see Frith 1991).

Difficulty with Receptive Language

Children with autism spectrum disorders sometimes have holes in their comprehension of vocabulary that cannot be explained in terms of developmental age. In many cases, this qualitative impairment is accompanied by a genuine delay in the development of comprehension as measured by objective testing. Such a delay may exist even where the child seems superficially to have no problem talking or understanding in the course of everyday life. This is because these children are often successful at using their memories of what "worked" in similar situations in the past, as well as visual cues gleaned from the current situation, to decide on the appropriate thing to do or say. As a result, they appear to have better comprehension than they actually do.

In order to provide children with the support they need, it is necessary to assess accurately their true level of language development (i.e., to find out whether or not they have a delay; for more on this, please refer to page 110, "Accurately Determining your Child's Language Comprehension Level"). Below I will discuss the most common types of qualitative impairments in language comprehension found in early childhood.

UNDERSTANDING LESS THAN THEY CAN SPEAK

With children on the high-functioning end of the autism spectrum, one should assume that they do not understand others as well as their ability to express themselves suggests.

Even babies who cannot talk yet will turn when their name is called; if they are hungry and a caregiver says, "Time for some yum-yums!" they will understand and look pleased. In typical development, the number of words a child understands is greater than the number of words he or she can say. This is only natural, because having the power of expression implies being able to form new linguistic constructions using vocabulary and grammar that have already been accumulated (in the form of receptive language). In direct contrast, however, children with ASDs often understand fewer words and sentences than they are capable of uttering. There are several reasons for this.

First, memorizing and reproducing words does not require comprehension. Children with ASDs may remember a sentence as a fixed sequence of words paired with a certain situation and can use this sentence correctly when speaking, but may be completely confused if someone then changes the order of the words just slightly.

Second, listening comprehension requires the processing of non-visual information in real time at a speed selected by the speaker. This can be very difficult for people with ASDs. Many on the spectrum may fail to understand something spoken, but then understand easily if the same words are written down verbatim. (Of course, this applies only to children who can already read and associate text with meaning.) Speaking, in contrast, is often easier because the child can process information at his or her own pace and may even compose sentences in his or her mind as if they were "written words." Temple Grandin (mentioned earlier) describes herself as a visual thinker who mentally processes information in the form of images (this is discussed in her book *Thinking in Pictures*; Grandin 1997).

Other factors contributing to the phenomenon of having more speech than comprehension can include difficulty inferring meaning from context and an intense interest in phonology (both discussed below). Some elementary school children with autism spectrum disorders are able to express what they experience as a result of their condition, and such children have occasionally confided to me that they "know all the words [their] friends are using but still can't piece together what they are saying."

SKEWED VOCABULARY

Many children with ASDs tend, from an early age, to have skewed vocabularies, such that compared with their peers they may know more words—particularly concrete nouns—in subjects that interest them, but at the same time have insufficient knowledge of verbs or words that express concepts.

Even concerning the words that they do know, these youngsters may have unique misunderstandings about their meaning. Some children, for example, may think that the word "flower" means "red tulip" or that "to go along with" means "to travel a far distance." This second example is somewhat related to the issue of phonology.

EXCESSIVE FOCUS ON PHONOLOGY

Several high-functioning children with ASDs have told me about experiences where they completely lose the thread of a conversation because they become fixated on an irrelevant phonological detail. One example I've heard is where the child was asked, "Can I go over to your house to play?" [*kimi-no* (=your) *uchi* (=house)], but the child became so distracted by images of farmland [*nouchi* (=farmland)] that the conversation stopped short.

In typical development, once the meaning of a piece of information has been recognized, the mind becomes constrained within the boundaries of that meaning, and any incongruous information (whether visual or auditory) tends not to register easily. Herein lies the challenge of anagrams (such as "fired calm," which can be decoded to form the words "fried clam"), or picture games such as "Spot the Difference"—especially in places where the differences are not highly pertinent to the overall scene. Perhaps the best way to describe this process is that we prioritize and add shading to individual pieces of information so that each piece becomes a unique component; when all the components are put together, we have a single, integrated meaning. The tendency of the brain to function this way is an obstacle when we attempt to solve puzzles such as those illustrated above (which is precisely why they're called "puzzles"), but it has the advantage of helping us to grasp ordinary meaning in our everyday lives by drawing our attention to the most relevant details. Uta Frith calls this intellectual function "central coherence" and has discussed it in relation to autism spectrum disorders (Happé 1997).

People with ASDs are said to have "weak central coherence"—that is, difficulty prioritizing and organizing individual bits of

information according to relevance. Consequently, they may get very high scores on picture completion tests (sections on IQ tests that ask, "What's missing from this picture?") or, conversely, very low scores because they cannot divert their attention away from details of particular interest. The same can be said concerning sound. It seems that people on the autism spectrum are able to enjoy phonology more freely, without being constrained by meaning. There are some people with HFA or AS, from elementary school age and upward, who can spout puns non-stop (at times to the point of becoming annoying). But sometimes, as illustrated at the beginning of this section, they become so caught up in sound that they lose track of meaning; their thoughts become fixed on specific sounds, and they become preoccupied with homonyms (e.g., hear/here) or amusing sound-alike pairs (e.g., chicken and gravy/kissing the baby).

DIFFICULTY INFERRING MEANING FROM CONTEXT

It is quite common in conversation to omit words from sentences. In such cases, the listener automatically infers the meaning from the context, and the conversation flows smoothly. For example, let's say I have been talking with Michitaka about kindergarten and have just asked him, "What kindergarten do you go to?" and "What class are you in?" Next, I say "Please tell me the name of your sensei" [a Japanese word that can mean either teacher or doctor]. A typically developing child would, without hesitation, tell me his kindergarten teacher's name. But Michitaka instead states my name – and he is not alone, as other children who have autism spectrum disorders often do the same. Similarly, they may answer the telephone and when asked, "Is your mother there?" respond, "Yes, she is" but not pass the telephone to her. Such a response is not mistaken in terms of vocabulary or grammar, but the children in these cases are interpreting the caller's words literally and are thus unable to infer the intended meaning, which would generally be considered obvious: "Please pass the phone to your mother, because I'd like to speak with her."

Children who interpret words literally often take jokes seriously. At the beginning of January, for example, when the traditional gift envelopes containing New Year's money are handed out to the children, if a father says, "You're so lucky. I wish I was a kid so I could get New Year's money, too," his son might admonish him quite seriously, telling him that it is impossible for him to become a child again. To take another example, elementary school children often tease each other in a friendly way, but children with ASDs may feel hurt or angry. And if you teach them that this kind of give-and-take among classmates is affectionate, they may use it themselves with someone they are not yet friends with and annoy them, or they may misinterpret actual insults as an expression of friendship.

DIFFICULTY UNDERSTANDING IDIOMS

People with ASDs also find it difficult to acquire idioms. One kindergarten child burst into tears when his teacher said, "You're so cute I'd like to eat you," and begged her not to eat him. An elementary school student, when told to "go straight home" responded with, "I have to turn in order to get to my house," earning the teacher's dislike for what she thought was impertinence. A junior high school student who was told "let's wipe the slate clean" began looking doubtfully for a blackboard.

Trouble understanding idioms is of course related to difficulty in acquiring common sense (an impairment of social interaction) and in inferring meaning from context (an impairment of communication), but considering that people can generally guess, to some extent, the meanings of idioms encountered in the study of a foreign language, it seems logical to assume that it is also related to an impairment of social imagination. As idioms are a product of "rules" (i.e., are determined by convention), they can be taught when the timing is right. Sometimes children on the spectrum begin to recognize that there seems to be a lot they don't understand and begin looking for keys to unlock the world's secrets, so to speak. At this stage, they may seize upon idiom dictionaries for this purpose and become engrossed in them; one pitfall of this strategy is that the dictionary might become a vehicle for pedantry, with the child learning and using idioms that would not be used by his or her peers.

Difficulty with Nonverbal Communication

Children with ASDs also have problems with both the use (expression) and comprehension (reception) of nonverbal means of communication, including the movement of the eyes in a particular direction, facial expressions, whole-body movements, or gesturing with the hands. Intonation and tone of voice are also usually included within the category of nonverbal communication.

These forms of communication are a useful basis for diagnosis in the case of babies and toddlers, but from kindergarten through primary school, when verbal communication begins to develop rapidly among all children, nonverbal communication is less of an issue. In adolescence, oddities in the use of body language begin to stand out and may be one factor in giving a teenager the overall appearance of being eccentric.

DIFFICULTY WITH EYE CONTACT AND OTHER COMMUNICATIVE EYE MOVEMENTS

People frequently observe that those with autism spectrum disorders have trouble making eye contact, but this difficulty should not be exaggerated. The fact is that one would be hard pressed to find even a single child with an ASD who has never once made eye contact. High-functioning children, especially, will usually be able to return the gaze of a person they know well and with whom they feel safe and secure. Some may have learned that they "should" look at the other person and as a result will not avert their glance for a moment, even when bowing in greeting. Even adults with Asperger's Syndrome can find it quite difficult to moderate their gaze when looking at other people. If a person to whom they have been paying no notice begins to speak, they will stare directly into the person's eyes from the start of the conversation to the finish, making him or her feel very uncomfortable.

It is also difficult for people with ASDs to understand what a look means. When our hands are full, we may use our eyes to indicate "over there," but this message is extremely difficult for them to take in. Some children do not even realize that there is information to be found at the place where the glance is directed. And even after they get this far, they still cannot understand looks that are meant to serve as signals, recognize surprise or censure expressed with the eyes, or realize that downcast eyes may mean that a person is not sleepy but rather embarrassed or insecure. Naturally, it is also difficult for them to use their eyes to send such messages to others. Difficulty communicating thoughts or feelings via the eyes is also a manifestation of impaired social development.

PROBLEMS WITH POINTING

The developmental histories of children with autism spectrum disorders often indicate that there was a lack of, or a delay in the appearance of, pointing in early childhood. Some parents of children on the high-functioning end of the spectrum, however, say that they did not notice any difficulty in this area when their children were little. As with eye contact, pointing should not be assessed merely on the basis of whether it occurs or not; rather, the content of communication for which pointing is used should be carefully examined.

In typical development, babies will begin pointing at things they are interested in before they reach the age of one. Pointing at this stage is self-contained, involving only the child and the object. Without any instruction, however, the function of pointing rapidly develops. Next, they begin to point at people in order to demand things; this is followed by their pointing not because they want something but because they are trying to share information or feelings. To elaborate, a baby at this stage will discover something wonderful and then want to share the enjoyment of this discovery with someone else. To this end, he or she will point at the object and then turn to look for a caregiver. When the caregiver responds, "Yes? What did you find?" the baby will, as if intending to show or explain, continue to point and also meet the caregiver's gaze. The practice of using nonverbal cues, such as pointing and looking, to attract another's attention to something of interest is technically known as "joint attention." In children with neurotypical development, joint attention emerges on its own by the age of one and a half. In children with ASDs, however, this behavior does not emerge readily or is exhibited in odd ways.

There are also some people on the spectrum who point excessively at everything or everyone. By the end of elementary school, typically developing children have come to realize, without being taught, that pointing at people is rude. They somehow know that pointing is only acceptable in very specific situations—such as when a teacher points at a student or when Detective Conan[4] is accusing a suspect of a crime.

People with ASDs also have a hard time discerning the meaning when another person is pointing. They may not realize that there is information to be found by looking to see where the finger is pointed and may instead concentrate on the finger itself, or they may follow the direction of the finger but be unable to find what it is pointing at. Let's say Dad is looking at his newspaper and suddenly points, saying, "Get that for me, will you?" Nearby family members will first formulate a guess in their minds (e.g., "He wants his glasses") and only then begin searching. People with ASDs may have trouble making this mental leap partly because they have difficulty with inferring meaning from context. (Other possible factors include difficulty with visual tracking and difficulty picking a particular object out from among numerous objects that are simultaneously competing for the person's attention.)

DIFFICULTY SUPPLEMENTING SPEECH WITH BODY LANGUAGE

People from other countries often say that Japanese people use little body language; they also apparently perceive us as lacking in facial expression. Indeed, as with pointing, few Japanese parents voice concern about the lack of or inappropriate facial expressions or other

---

4   A popular Japanese cartoon hero, Detective Conan is an elementary school boy/ crime detective who always points and says, "You're the criminal!" when he solves a case.

types of body language except during very early childhood or from puberty on. But when we meet someone with an autism spectrum disorder, even someone who is high functioning, something about his appearance will almost always strike us as incongruous. If we stop to think about why, we will realize how important a role body language actually plays, even in Japanese communication. I believe that Japanese people do not actually lack facial expressiveness, but rather that we make distinctions within a narrower range. With regard to all types of body language—including facial expression, gestures, and whole-body movements and positioning—I think that we, as a culture, do in fact have a limit below which we perceive expressiveness to be impoverished; at the same time, we also have a limit above which we see expressiveness to be excessive, and this limit just happens to be stricter than that employed by Westerners. Particularly in the case of high-functioning children with autism spectrum disorders, it is easier to diagnose inappropriate or excessive expression than it is to spot a lack of expression.

For example, many children with Kanner's Syndrome give the impression of being expressionless, whereas children with Asperger's Syndrome often exhibit childlike expressions. Some of the latter may constantly wear a slight smile. They may have been taught that this expression is "appropriate" (i.e., easier to get through life with), but to the extent that they smile even when unhappy, we must conclude that they have a qualitative impairment. Exaggerated, off-the-shelf facial expressions or gestures, such as those used by child actors in old films, are also common. When it is time to smile, the corners of their mouths jerk upwards as if pulled by strings and they flash a bright Hollywood smile as if a switch has been turned on. Or when they are happy, they put their hands to their cheeks in a rapturous pose. Other examples of unnatural body language include placing a finger to the forehead with furrowed brow (while deep in thought) or standing with arms crossed and head tilted; clearly these poses are out of sync with the image of a typical kindergarten or elementary school child. Such children will also often grin when they are distressed.

Children on the high-functioning end of the spectrum may never use body language that is conspicuously inappropriate; when they do, this behavior usually corrects itself sometime during early childhood. One example of an error that may or may not be seen in very young children is that of waving with the palm turned inward instead of outward. Mistakes of this kind are thought to reflect a difficulty in learning patterns that require adjusting the model being imitated to account for a difference in perspective (speaker vs. listener, person waving vs. person being waved to).

From adolescence onwards, when other children begin supplementing verbal communication with a socially appropriate repertoire of subtle facial expressions, gestures, and body positions, oddness in this area of communication once again becomes apparent. When a person stands tall with his head back, he gives people the impression that he is either arrogant or angry. Leaning forward when listening indicates interest in what the other person has to say and generates a feeling of closeness. People with ASDs, even high-functioning adults, however, find it very difficult to appropriately use or understand such body language. Nonverbal methods of communication add depth and resonance to a conversation. Two people enjoying an animated discussion about a certain subject will automatically and wordlessly carry that feeling of enjoyment into the rest of the conversation, even after the topic

has changed. This experience is very rare, however, in conversations with high-functioning people on the autism spectrum.

EXAMPLES OF BEHAVIORS COMMONLY SEEN IN EARLY CHILDHOOD

On the high-functioning end of the autism spectrum, there are indications that certain qualitative impairments of communication exist even as early as babyhood (although broad questioning of the type, "Did the child ever point, or not?" often fails to yield this type of information).

In typical development, babies enjoy communication with their mothers even before they can speak. They will babble enthusiastically, as if conversing with her. When they want to be picked up, they will hold their hands out towards her and vocalize. Rather than simply reaching out to touch her, they appear to be quite aware that this gesture is a "signal" (i.e., a form of language). Similarly, they quickly become adept at pointing without anyone having to teach them. By the time they are about one year old, they will respond to the words, "Bye-bye" by facing the speaker and waving, even if no one is modelling this behavior for them at that moment. At the next stage, children will wave on their own initiative when it's time to leave or when they have had enough of a particular activity. In children on the autism spectrum, however, this pattern of development is less common, or else its manifestation includes eccentricities—again, such as waving with the palm facing inward instead of outward.

It is not uncommon for even high-functioning individuals with ASDs to have exhibited delayed language development during early childhood, although some do in fact say their first words at the usual age. Even in these latter instances, it is often discovered that there was a qualitative impairment in language acquisition somewhere along the way. As explained on page 43 in the section "Difficulty with Expressive Language," it is not unusual to see certain biases in the type of vocabulary people with ASDs acquire. In typical development, children begin using two-word sentences around the age of two only after their vocabulary has increased to between fifty and one hundred words and they have been both comprehending and using single words for some time. In children on the autism spectrum, first words and the emergence of two-word sentences often appear quite close together. It has also been frequently reported that these children may almost entirely skip the stage of using single words to communicate and instead suddenly begin uttering a limited range of two-word sentences.

Some parents also tell me that, as babies, their children did not look at them when nursing (whether they were breastfed or bottle-fed), did not turn and make eye contact when their names were called, or lacked facial expression. Occasionally, however, I encounter children with Asperger's Syndrome or other milder forms of ASDs who either never exhibited any of these deficits or else seemed to overcome them for the most part before the age of two.

Qualitative Impairment of Social Imagination

The word "imagination" usually brings to mind artistic creativity, but here it is used in a broader sense to mean the ability to visualize something that is not actually in front of you. And not only to visualize, but also to think, "Maybe it is like this or maybe it is like that." People with an impairment of imagination have difficulty enjoying the unknown or responding flexibly and appropriately to unexpected outcomes. They prefer the familiar and tend to be biased in favor of outcomes that reflect their interests.

A Different Sort of Make-believe Play

It is not possible to assess the ability of toddlers to intuitively deal with abstract concepts, causal relationships, or the realm of possibility. However, Lorna Wing identified lack of make-believe play as a precursor to difficulty in this area.

In typical development, children begin to enjoy imitative play that follows a pattern from the age of about one and a half. A child will raise an empty cup, tap it against his mother's, say "Cheers!" and pretend to drink. He smiles happily, experiencing the feeling that this little act has been shared. This type of pretend play develops rapidly without any instruction, and by the time the child is about three he begins to enjoy playing make-believe games with a story and different people playing different roles. Among children of ages four or five, make-believe games that evolve through everyone's participation are popular. By this age, repetition of the same storyline is considered boring. The thrill of make-believe lies in reciprocity (interaction with others) and the development of variations as a result of that interaction. The children are fully aware that the events taking place are fictitious, and they know that they can return to reality at any time, but it is the shared choice to remain in that fantasy world together that makes it fun.

In contrast, children on the autism spectrum often show no interest in playing make-believe, or else they start when they are older. Moreover, their make-believe games are qualitatively different from those of children with neurotypical development: they are difficult for others to share, do not easily evolve through interaction with others, and may have unusual boundaries between reality and fantasy. Some children with ASDs will say that playing "house" is their favorite leisure time activity, but in the majority of cases it would be more apt to call their version of this game a "memory re-enactment." When they do engage in pretend play with other children, they may be merely following the instructions of a "boss" or, in contrast, only seeking out "friends" who are willing to take direction down to the last detail, including all of the lines they are to say. Often children on the spectrum are completely immersed in a fantasy world. Some continue to enjoy producing, directing, and acting in endless one-man shows no matter how old they are, or they may at all times adopt the persona—including poses, voice, and so on—of a particular superhero or cartoon character. Some children even speak to invisible characters as if they were really there, but this behavior is merely an extreme form of fantasizing and is not the same as hallucinating.

Difficulty Experiencing the Joy of Anticipation

Imagine you are a child and a present arrives from your grandmother, who lives in the countryside. As you pick up the box, you wonder what's inside. "Could it be the PlayStation I asked for? It's a little small for that. Maybe it's a Game Boy! Oh, but what if it's just a box of pencils?" You are filled with excitement and anticipation until you finally get to see what's inside. Your imagination is free to roam, and your enjoyment is amplified precisely because you don't know what the contents are. Children with neurotypical development are able to experience and enjoy the feeling of anticipation by the age of four or five at the latest. This is the power of social imagination.

But children on the autism spectrum find such situations difficult. Rather than feeling excited, they tend to become anxious or agitated. Some may arbitrarily decide what the contents are going to be because they are uncomfortable with the situation. And if the reality differs from what they have ordained, they may become confused or angry. Parents often feel annoyed by the child's wilful suppositions and resultant anger. It is much easier to understand the feelings of such children if you have some knowledge about impairment of imagination.

Trouble Switching Gears

Once children on the autism spectrum have their minds set on something, they find it very hard to make adjustments. This includes revising assumptions about the "uncertain future," such as those seen in the previous example, as well as changing the order of steps in a task that is under way. They may devise certain ways of coping with the need to make changes, such as by going back to the very beginning when they make a wrong turn in a maze or by erasing an entire page and starting over when they have made a single mistake. Switching gears emotionally may also be difficult once their feelings have been stirred up.

They tend to make incorrect assumptions that they then find hard to turn away from. Life can be more difficult both for them and for family members if this tendency is not understood. Trouble switching gears can manifest itself in many different ways. Some children may show it outwardly by becoming angry or contrary, while others may do as they are told but feel anxious or frustrated inside. With children in the latter category, teachers and parents may make the mistake of frequently demanding that they accept change flexibly because they don't seem to have trouble coping with such expectations. If a child exhibits other characteristics of impaired imagination yet appears not to have difficulty shifting his thinking, I suggest you look again more closely to see whether this assessment is accurate. Does the child seem to be keeping up with activities but appear anxious or uncomfortable? Does he keep his emotions in check when this is required at kindergarten or school, but then show his pent up distress at home? Is his attachment to perseverative behaviors increasing? Is he suffering from insomnia, does he bite his nails, or does he have tics that are becoming more pronounced? One harmless way to assess whether a child has difficulty switching gears is to provide supports for this purpose and observe changes in facial expression and behavior: if the child becomes more relaxed, you can assume that he was previously having difficulty. (For suggested supports, see page 137, "The Ability to Switch Emotional Gears.")

Taking Comfort in the Familiar

Children who have an impairment of social imagination feel very relaxed and secure when things unfold according to their expectations and, in such situations, they are able to fully demonstrate their natural abilities. In contrast, they may become so agitated at school events that are held only occasionally, such as Sports Day or Parents' Observation Day, that they cannot even do things they would usually manage very well. Or a slight adjustment to the daily kindergarten routine, such as not changing into uniform play smocks first thing in the morning, can seem like a bolt of lightning out of the blue and throw them into a panic. Even on family trips or summer vacations, many children prefer making

the usual visit to their grandparents' house or staying at the same hotel as always because they find new places exhausting. Schedules are used as a support for children with autism spectrum disorders (see page 140, "Deriving Power from Transparency") not to control or manipulate them, but rather to make situations predictable, which puts them at ease and better enables them to attempt various activities and realize their full potential.

Confused by the Unexpected

It is very difficult for children on the autism spectrum to think flexibly or adapt their behavior appropriately when things happen that they have not been expecting; social imagination is essential when one is trying something new. Facing the unexpected fills these children with panic and reduces their usual information-processing ability even further, making confusion an inevitable consequence.

You should probably prepare yourself for the fact that children with ASDs will tend to have meltdowns in the face of the unexpected and that this type of response will continue even after they reach physical maturity. But think of the child's memory as a drawer. As the child goes through various life experiences and the drawer is filled with more and more information and behavioral procedures, the number of "unexpected" situations he or she meets will decrease, and so, too, will the occurrence and intensity of confusion.

Difficulty Making Predictions

Children on the autism spectrum who are at a low level of development (either because of an intellectual disability or because they are still very young) find it difficult to understand causal relationships. Some children, for example, do not understand such simple physical principles as the fact that if they throw something away, they will no longer have it, or that if they drop something, it might break. Those on the high end of the spectrum generally do understand visible and concrete relationships such as these and are also able to predict that in similar situations they will get the same results if they repeat an action. They have trouble, however, predicting outcomes in situations that they have never experienced. As explained in the section on communication (page 50, "Difficulty Considering What Others Are Thinking"), such children find it hard to gauge other people's intentions or feelings. Many children on the spectrum do not fully grasp what it means to predict the results of an action before they perform it. It may seem that if only they could envision and anticipate a variety of possible outcomes, they could avoid the discomfort of dealing with the unexpected. Unfortunately, though, the lack of vision and the discomfort both come from the same place—an impairment of social imagination—and, naturally, the greater the difficulty with making predictions, the more unanticipated outcomes the child will have to face.

There are also some children who rely on set patterns to decide from the outset what an end result will be. For example, they may believe everything they see on TV or read in a book, or they may be convinced that an outcome they experienced previously is going to be repeated. Such misconceptions also increase the likelihood of encountering the unexpected.

Unwillingness to Try Something New

Children with impaired social imagination do not like new challenges. They will only attempt something unfamiliar after watching several other children do it first, even if the activity is within their capability. If offered a new food, they will usually refuse it. When a child is unwilling to try something new, it is not enough just to consider whether the task is too difficult or whether he or she may be confused about what to do because of an impairment in communication; we must also consider the possibility that he or she is being hindered by an impairment of imagination. Refusal that arises from the latter limits the child's range of experience. But it is dangerous to blindly insist that he or she try something just for that reason, because such insistence fails to recognize the existence of a genuine disability. To get children who have ASDs to try new things, we must aim to create an even more relaxed and secure environment than would be necessary for typical children who do not have ASDs; to reassure them that it is safe to try, we need to provide them with visual clues as to what the experience entails and how it is likely to unfold.

Even children on the autism spectrum can love novelty as long as they are sure it will not disrupt their lives. Their avid thirst for knowledge is proof of this. Some are very happy to take a different route every time they go for a drive once they know that they will always return home at the end. Rather than having an aversion to everything that is new, it may just be that they are afraid of the unpredictable—of circumstances where the impact on their lives is unknown.

Inability to Extract and Apply Principles

Let's say a typical child has been taught to eat everything on his plate. Today, his family is visiting Grandma, and she serves him more than he can handle. He will realize at some level that this situation may be an exception to the rule observed at home, and so he will ask, "May

I leave some?" The same child will know instinctively, without being told, that he is not supposed to eat everything on the large serving dishes at a buffet table. Impairment of social imagination, however, impedes the ability to extract principles learned in one situation and apply them appropriately in another. This means that a child who has been taught to eat everything on his plate may approach the dinner table with a do-or-die resolve to finish every last bite on a day when he is actually not feeling well.

Children on the autism spectrum therefore find it difficult to extract principles, rules, and essential characteristics or points in common from concrete and individual circumstances. When asked on an IQ test, for example, "What is a hat?" such children may respond by describing the characteristics of their own hat: "The black thing with the New York Yankees emblem on it." Although they have seen a great variety of hats during their lifetime, and even just at day care, they have trouble formulating the concept of what, in general, constitutes a hat.

Children with an impaired social imagination may also generalize excessively and be convinced that these generalizations form a set of self-made laws. Adults with Asperger's Syndrome sometimes have problems in personal relationships because they are sure that their own experiences are tantamount to principles and rules that apply to everybody (or at least to everybody with Asperger's Syndrome). The tendency that school-age children have to arbitrarily decide outcomes (see page 69) is a similar phenomenon.

Inclination toward Order

Children with an impaired social imagination will seek to maintain their own unique version of sameness, or familiarity. The content of the "order" that they insist upon is very diverse. It may involve where or how certain objects are to be placed (all edges lined up, for example); bedtime rituals; demanding that doors must always be closed; or always walking on the curb when outside. Some high-functioning children on the autism spectrum sift out any rules that noticeably interfere with daily life and, consequently, they appear not to have any rules. It may only be when the water heater is broken that a child's parents realize the importance to him or her of the ritual of an after-dinner bath.[5] Some parents of elementary and junior high school children with Asperger's Syndrome are convinced that their children do not have this preoccupation with order, but when the children themselves are asked, they will say that in fact they prefer when things are always done the same way.

The degree to which children have trouble deferring to others' wishes also varies. Some children will be so insistent on working through a certain procedure that being stopped will cause them to panic, while other children will stop if they are instructed to do so. Such perseverations are strongest between the ages of two and three, and the ability to defer to others gradually increases thereafter.

Children on the autism spectrum often acquire practical life habits that require repeating a sequence of actions—such as brushing their teeth or tidying up—even earlier than their typical peers. This is one positive manifestation of the strong inclination toward order.

---

5   In Japan, evening baths for all—including older children and adults—are more common than the Western custom of showering in the morning.

Wanting Others to Preserve Order

Some children try to extend their sense of order to others. For example, they may have decided where everyone in the family should sit at the table or the order in which the family should line up when they are walking together. They may also be very upset if someone in their class at school is absent. Again, the content and level of intolerance vary.

The insistence on a particular order of activity can disrupt everyday life in the household. A child may demand, for example, that his mother sit beside him whenever he looks at books and read out the titles of every book he points to—regardless of whatever else she may need to be doing at that moment.

Lack of Balance in Interests

Children on the autism spectrum tend to have strong and biased interests in specific things or subjects. Some examples include: vehicles and related paraphernalia (cars, trains, airplanes, and traffic signals and signs); insects; dinosaurs; things that turn; things that shine; blue things; things that form pairs; letters; numbers; television commercials; particular picture books or videos; the police; the military; boxes of laundry detergent (which, for some reason, seem to be somewhat popular); timetables; maps; and history. They may memorize related information and carry out simulations in their minds. Some children also have strong attachments to pop stars or to a particular classmate. Although children with ASDs exhibit countless varieties of interests like these—that is, ones that lack balance in the scheme of everyday life—strangely, the content tends to be similar from one country to another.

When the object of the child's interest is a video game, a pop star, or a TV program, it is difficult for parents to recognize it as stemming from an imbalance in the child's interests—but such a conclusion may be indicated if the interest is so narrow and intense that it precludes other forms of play. Biased interests can also be difficult to discern if the object of a child's interest changes over time, but again this possibility must be considered if the degree of interest is intense, or if the child's interests merely switch from one narrow area to another without any kind of spiral-like expansion.

A Preference for Memorizing, Collecting, and Arranging

Children who have ASDs often prefer games that involve repeating a certain sequence or organizing objects rather than activities that require thinking deeply about meaning. Young children or those who have intellectual disabilities will become engrossed in making rows of blocks or other objects, pressing toys that beep, or playing with toys where they can put balls into holes and watch them roll down. From early childhood, many on the high-functioning end of the autism spectrum enjoy collecting things or information. They may collect toy cars, memorize national flags, absorb information from a video game strategy manual, or buy all the books in a series and read them cover to cover. The age at which such children evince an interest in letters and begin memorizing them is often quite young.

Behaviors Common in Infancy

It is quite usual for typically developing babies to enjoy putting things in their mouth or pressing a button over and over. For this reason, it is difficult to discern impairments of social imagination at this age. However, if babies repeat behaviors indicative of sensory issues or certain movement-related behaviors, such as being transfixed by a fluttering curtain or a glittering leaf, entwining their fingers and staring at them for long periods without becoming bored, or repeatedly banging their head against their crib rails, then there is reason to suspect an impairment of social imagination. Unbalanced interests or habits cannot, by definition, appear until the child has enough intellect to remember what he has liked and done before, and therefore these characteristics are also not clearly evident in infancy. Some children under the age of one, however, have been reported to refuse to drink anything but a specific brand of formula or from any baby bottle that does not have a certain type of nipple; others of this age are said to show an unusually strong interest in trains or car license plates, or to enjoy looking at the telephone directory. In high-functioning children on the autism spectrum, unbalanced interests and habits usually become more and more apparent starting around the age of one and a half, or after the child has turned two. Other behaviors that have frequently been reported include obvious preferences for a specific route on outings, unusually strong interest in numbers, attachments to vehicles or TV characters (such as Thomas the Tank Engine or Batman), the tendency to continually hold a certain object, lining or piling up objects, spinning anything that will spin, and twirling anything long and thin.

Absorption in Stereotyped Movements or in Sensory Stimulation

Repetitive movements, such as twirling round and round, jumping up and down, flapping or waving both hands, rocking, tapping one's fingers, and so on, are common in young children with ASDs. These are called stereotyped movements, or stereotypies. So-called toe-walking (i.e., walking on tiptoe) is also a form of stereotypy. Sensory issues (see page 79) such as absorption in staring at things, putting things against the mouth, twirling a piece of string, smelling things, touching hair or stockings, and so on, are also common. In children with Asperger's Syndrome, absorption in stereotyped movements or sensory stimulation may be overlooked, or they may become less obvious from about the age of three.

It may be more appropriate to view these behaviors as problems with movement or sensation rather than as impairments of social imagination. However, the fact that they provide a sense of relaxation and retain the child's interest despite their repetitive quality indicates that these behaviors are related to flexibility.

2. Symptoms Outside of the Wing Triad

The symptoms discussed below are also common to many children on the autism spectrum. Their presence, however, does not influence diagnosis because not all children on the spectrum have them and because they can also occur in children who do not have ASDs. While not used as diagnostic criteria, these symptoms are still important, as they often prove to be the most disruptive to family life during early childhood.

Inattention/ADHD/Impulsivity

Children on the autism spectrum often feel anxious and confused in a new situation because of impaired social imagination, and this can cause them to lose their composure. Impairments in socialization or communication often make it difficult for them to understand what is expected of them, and they will get up and move around at the wrong times. They are frequently impulsive in their behavior: children who like police cars might dash off to get a close look (whatever the circumstances) if one happens by, while those who are Batman fans might be unable to resist expounding on the subject whenever it comes up. When preoccupied with their own interests, most are unable to pay attention to anything else. In general, such inattention, hyperactivity, and impulsivity can all be explained by the Wing triad.

In some cases, however, a child with an ASD will exhibit inattention, hyperactivity, and/or impulsivity to an extent or of a quality that cannot be explained by the Wing triad. It should be borne in mind that these particular symptoms are fundamental to the condition known as attention deficit hyperactivity disorder (ADHD), which I explain further beginning on page 93.

Issues Involving Movement and Motor Clumsiness

While a few children on the spectrum exhibit outstanding dexterity, many are clumsy in both their fine motor movements (e.g., use of the fingers, lips, tongue, throat, and facial muscles) and gross motor movements (e.g., use of the arms, legs, and torso). Many also lack the motor ability needed to maintain correct posture, having a tendency to go limp, and toe-walking (walking on tiptoe) is also common in younger children. Gillberg and Gillberg, of Sweden, include "motor clumsiness: poor performance on neuro-developmental examination" as a necessary criterion in the diagnosis of Asperger's Syndrome (see Appendix 1). While there has been some debate as to whether this inclusion is really necessary, it is certainly true that many children with AS are clumsy.

Parents should also know that some teens with ASDs may develop a symptom called catatonia, an impairment of mobility. Catatonia was first reported as a motor impairment that occurred following encephalitis, and it is known in adult psychiatry as a symptom strongly related to schizophrenia. Catatonia has received increasing attention as a symptom that frequently appears in adolescents and adults with ASDs since the publication of a report by Wing and Shah in 2000. Catatonia is characterized by a noticeable decrease in voluntary movement and includes stopping a movement in the middle or moving suddenly, like a compressed spring being released, curling the fingers, or walking back and forth on the same spot when trying to move forward. As this motor impairment is sometimes mistaken as a refusal to participate in activities or as a kind of "fooling around," it is important for parents and teachers of older children with ASDs to be aware of its existence.

Although many children on the spectrum do not show delays in early motor milestones—such as beginning to walk—some are examined by pediatric neurologists or pediatric physiotherapists for such motor-related concerns as delayed head control, delayed walking, or a tendency to fall. There are also cases in which an individual may be treated for cerebral palsy in early childhood, and after entering elementary school be additionally diagnosed with Asperger's Syndrome.

Peculiar Responses to Sensory Stimuli

Input via the five senses (sight, hearing, smell, touch, taste) needs to be recognized by the cerebrum. When we listen to a sound, for example, the ears do not function alone. The brain plays an important role in processing audio information. What we experience as "sound" results when air waves cause the eardrum to vibrate; this vibration is converted into an electrical impulse and conveyed to the cerebrum, and the information is then processed as "so much volume," "this kind of tone," and "a sound heard at that time." Because autism spectrum disorders are caused by certain characteristics in the brain, it is only natural that people on the spectrum will experience distortions in the processing of sensory stimuli.

One symptom frequently observed is sensitivity to sound. Some children wake easily or cry at noises from the time they are babies. They will have an excessive aversion to a particular noise or volume level and may cover their ears. Some children have very sharp hearing, but only for sounds they like, such as the sound of a bag of snacks being opened or a certain TV commercial. Usually in such children this hypersensitivity is coupled with hyposensitivity. They may be totally unperturbed by noises that make others cringe, such as a nail scraping on glass, or when concentrating they may remain oblivious to or respond very slowly to a loud noise occurring right beside them.

Peculiar responses to tactile stimuli range from hyper-sensitivity—for example, having an extreme aversion to touching clay or glue or to wearing certain fabrics (such as coarse cotton or acrylic)—to hyposensitivity—for instance, playing a game of dodgeball and not even being aware when the ball has brushed against one's clothing. In some cases, a child may show a marked preference for a particular type of tactile stimulus, always wanting, perhaps, to touch pantyhose or hair, to stroke a blanket or something furry, or to knead something with the fingertips.

Atypical responses to visual stimuli often reported in cases of children with ASDs include the following: being mesmerized by shiny objects or spinning objects; preferring to look at objects in a certain way, such as by squinting or looking out of the corner of their eye, through the fingers, or from different angles; and being highly sensitive to light for no apparent ophthalmologic reason.

Various other sensory behaviors and traits are also known to occur, such as sniffing odourless objects; frequently biting or mouthing various items; being hypersensitive or hyposensitive to pain, heat, or cold; and exhibiting excessive pleasure or extreme fear of vestibular stimuli (being raised high in the air or swinging).

It is important that people involved with children on the autism spectrum understand that such sensory peculiarities are derived from certain characteristics of the brain.

Difficulty with Visual Tasks

It is considered axiomatic that children on the autism spectrum are good at understanding information that is presented visually. It therefore may seem strange to hear that they have certain particular difficulties with visual tasks. And yet children on the spectrum—particularly those with Asperger's Syndrome—often have trouble finding one needed item when there are lots of other items surrounding it or comparing an object with a model and determining whether or not it is the same. In many children, this is coupled with difficulty in remembering letters, which suggests that this characteristic overlaps with the issue of learning difficulties (about which, see page 101). The inability to focus selectively on a specific target within a large amount of information is also related to attention deficit and possibly also to clumsy eye movements (difficulty with ocular pursuit, or visual tracking) and to distorted responses to visual stimuli. Although the precise reason for difficulty with visual tasks cannot be determined, we do know for certain that some children on the autism spectrum experience such difficulties.

One problem that arises from this paradox is the mistaken conclusion that presenting information visually is not effective for aiding understanding in such children. In fact, such visual supports are beneficial because they provide input in a form that is both non-auditory and durable. Even children who adequately understand speech find it helpful to have information in a form that—unlike spoken language—does not vanish as soon as it is presented. Input that remains visible can be grasped slowly, at the child's own pace, and checked again if the child becomes anxious or unsure. Children may find it a great relief simply to know that they can always look at the visual support if they lose track or find themselves not understanding.

If you do not see much effect after using a visual to explain something, I suggest assessing whether the presentation needs to be changed in some way to suit that particular child better. For example, rather than merely showing the child a picture, it may be necessary to circle the main point with a marker or write out the explanation in words. Even with the written word, you may need to consider limiting each item you present to an amount that will fit within the child's visual field; underlining important points may also be a key to success.

Bear in mind that visual supports may be falsely judged ineffective because of two common errors: (1) presenting visuals that are too "busy"—that is, containing too many stimuli in a disorganized manner that does not focus sufficiently on the main point, and (2) using picture or word cards with a child who has not yet reached a level of development where these can be comprehended.

Eating Behavior Problems

Problems with eating habits often cause parents of infants, toddlers, and school-age children much concern. These range from extreme pickiness to rejecting foods with certain textures, such as deep-fried foods, to gagging on anything that is gooey or sticky, to wanting things that people generally do not eat (such as roasted coffee beans) or that are usually preferred by adults (such as sharp pickles, anchovies, or strong cheeses). Some of these difficulties are the result of biases in taste or texture. To the extent that the problems are due to unusual characteristics of the brain, they will often become less obvious as the child grows older and the brain matures. Please see page 186 for more information on this subject.

Sleep Problems

Most newborn babies spend most of the day sleeping. Gradually, however, their sleeping hours become confined to two blocks of time, one at night and one during the day, and then finally to night time only. As the establishment of this sleep pattern is related to maturation of the brain, it is quite common for children with developmental disabilities such as autism to have sleep-related problems. They may sleep very little and even after they become toddlers may not fall asleep at a regular hour or may wake up frequently during the night. The section "Helping Daily Life Run Smoothly" describes steps that can be taken to deal with insomnia (page 191).

III. Other Medical Information

This section offers additional medical information for parents of young children with high-functioning ASDs.

Autism Spectrum Disorders are Not Unusual

The first statistics on the morbidity rate for autism (the percentage of a population with autism) were presented by Victor Lotter in a report on an epidemiological study of children in England (Lotter 1966). The total prevalence given in his report was only 4.5 per 10,000, and consequently autism was thought to be a rare disability. Subsequently, Lorna Wing and Judith Gould came up with an estimate of 20 per 10,000, in which they included those who had IQs of under 70 and the Wing triad of impairments but who did not fit definitions of autism generally recognized at that time (Wing and Gould 1979). In consideration of this and other studies, at the time the National Autistic Society of the United Kingdom calculated 91 per 10,000 as the official estimate for the prevalence of ASDs (20 per 10,000 for those with IQs under 70 plus 71 per 10,000 for those with IQs above 70) (see www.autism.org.uk/7874). In Sweden, Kadesjo, Gillberg and Hagberg (1999) reported a prevalence for ASDs of 121 per 10,000, of which 70 percent had IQs of over 70. In the United Kingdom, one study (Baird et al. 2000) reported a prevalence of 31 per 10,000 for autism and 58 per 10,000 for the entire spectrum; in a later study (Baird et al. 2006), these same researchers cited a prevalence of 39 per 10,000 for autism and 116 per 10,000 for the entire spectrum. The average IQ for those on the spectrum was 69.4 (a person with an IQ of 70 or above is considered not to have an intellectual impairment). Japan, where the nationwide system of regular infant and child health checkups is unparalleled, was the first country to recognize a relatively high incidence of Kanner's Syndrome, reporting a morbidity rate for this disorder of 13 to 21 per 10,000 (Ishii and Takahashi 1983; Honda *et al.* 1996; Sugiyama and Abe 1989).

The above studies suggest that as many as one in every hundred children may well have some form of ASD, making this set of disorders far from rare. Moreover, in 60 to 70 percent of cases the disorders are not accompanied by intellectual disabilities. Looking only at mainstream classrooms, if there are 150 children registered per grade at any given school, there is bound to be at least one person with an ASD in each grade. Educational intervention for affected students thus cannot be dismissed by any kindergarten or school in any community as "not our concern."

The prevalence of autism spectrum disorders has heretofore been reported as four or five times higher for boys than for girls. But there is growing recognition that if children with milder cases are included, the prevalence among girls is actually higher than previously thought. This is an impression shared by those of us in clinical practice as well.

Kathy Hoopmann has written an excellent series of children's novels where Asperger's Syndrome is a central theme. Although the main character, Ben, is a boy, the narrator in one of the three volumes, Lisa, is a girl, and she has Asperger's Syndrome (Hoopmann 2002). This may reflect the fact that more girls are being brought in for consultations because of concerns about symptoms associated with ASDs.

Setback Phenomenon

Children on the autism spectrum sometimes appear to be developing in a typical manner and then experience stagnation or regression. This is known as the "setback phenomenon." This phenomenon is most frequently noticed when a child's vocabulary declines, but it may also be seen in various other areas of development: the child may cease to make eye contact or suddenly begin to have difficulty doing so; he or she may also stop laughing or smiling, or stop engaging in imitative behavior. Although precise numbers depend on what is defined as a "setback," reports indicate that about one-third of all children with autism spectrum disorders exhibit this phenomenon.

In the majority of cases, the setback begins between the ages of eighteen months and two and a half years. Sometimes there seems to be no precipitating cause, but many times some event marks the beginning of a turn toward sluggish development. This age range very often coincides with the birth of a sibling, a job transfer for younger couples, or a move into a new house. As a consequence, the setback is often seen as a temporary response to stressful circumstances and consultation is delayed. Awareness must be increased that just because a child does not appear to experience any developmental problems up to age one and a half does not rule out the possibility that he or she may have an ASD.

It must be questioned whether the development of children diagnosed with setback phenomena could truly be called "typical" before the setback occurred; when interviewed during consultations, many parents will recall that when very young their children showed no stranger anxiety, made no attempt to imitate hand movements during action songs, or showed other behavior indicative of mild

qualitative difficulties in development, even though the parents did not recognize these behaviors as reasons for concern at the time.

As a general rule, the setback phenomenon does not include regression in motor development. If you observe any regression in walking, hand use, and so on, you should immediately consult a pediatric neurologist, as these symptoms could be indications of a neurological disease.

The Autism Spectrum and Epileptic Seizures

It is known that about 20 percent of children with autism (Kanner's Syndrome) also suffer from epilepsy, a condition typified by repeated seizures, including convulsions and loss of consciousness, that are caused by abnormal electrical discharges from brain cells. If epilepsy is present, "paroxysmal abnormality" will frequently show up on electroencephalograms (EEGs). Research reports up to the present have noted that the tendency towards epileptic seizures increases with the severity of mental disability. Considering the fact that the more pronounced the autistic symptoms and mental disabilities of an individual, the greater the brain disorder, this would seem to make sense. Yet when examining children at the treatment centre attended by the majority of children with autism spectrum disorders in my local area, including even very mild cases, I have found that a surprising number of children with high-functioning autism and Asperger's Syndrome have epileptic seizures. There is no denying the possibility that some children who are being treated for epilepsy alone may also have HFA or AS that is going unrecognized, with their seizures acting as a red herring.

The epileptic seizures of most children who have mild mental disabilities and are on the autism spectrum can be controlled relatively easily with proper medication, and therefore there is no need to worry about the possibility of such seizures before they occur.

The most common age range during which children on the autism spectrum experience their first seizures is adolescence (junior to senior high school), followed by the period from ages four to seven, around the time a child starts kindergarten or elementary school. Abnormalities begin to show up on EEGs from around the age of ten. While EEGs administered to children at age two or three (for the purpose of making a thorough diagnosis) often show nothing unusual, it is worth having them done periodically as one method of grasping the condition of the child's brain. It is a good idea to have an EEG done at least once a year if anything notable has been identified; if not, it should be sufficient to have the test performed around the time of entrance to elementary school and then once more just before or after the transition to middle school.

The Autism Spectrum and Heredity

It is not yet clear what causes the brain characteristics that give rise to autism spectrum disorders. While the presence of the behavioral characteristics that constitute the Wing triad (see page 33) forms the basis for diagnosing ASDs, there are believed to be a range of possible causes, so any two individuals with the same diagnosis may have acquired their disorders by different means. In addition, several factors may be related to the emergence of an ASD even within the same individual.

The National Autistic Society (NAS) has worked hard to promote awareness of autism spectrum disorders and provides a variety of medical and psychological information on its website. The NAS outlook on the cause of autism is described below.

What Causes Autism?

> The causes of ASDs are still being investigated. Many experts believe
> that the pattern of behaviour from which an ASD is diagnosed may not
> result from a single cause. There is strong evidence to suggest that ASDs
> can be caused by a variety of physical factors, all of which affect brain
> development. ASDs are not due to emotional deprivation or the way a
> person has been brought up.
>
> There is evidence to suggest that genetic factors are responsible for
> some forms of ASD. An ASD is likely to be caused by several genes
> interacting rather than by one single gene. For some years, scientists have
> been attempting to identify which genes might be implicated in ASDs.
> (National Autistic Society 2012)

In keeping with its recognition of the significance of heredity, the
NAS provides support for genetic research and recruits families
willing to participate in such research. In contrast, in Japan
information concerning genetic factors is treated differently from
other types of medical information: experts in the medical profession
avoid speaking frankly about heredity, distancing parents from that
kind of data. But we as parents and medical professionals all need to
focus on seeking the facts concerning the autism spectrum. Surely
we need to empower ourselves with any available information and
use it wisely.

My own impression is that the term "hereditary" is often misunderstood. Genetic factors contributing to disease represent
a predisposition. For example, people on identical diets respond
differently. One may gain weight while another does not, one may
become diabetic while another does not, and one may get high
blood pressure whereas another does not. A person genetically

predisposed to acquiring diabetes may or may not actually get the disease; the outcome will depend on other factors, with severe stress, for example, sometimes acting as a trigger.

Even before medical science began to prove that diseases were partly hereditary (i.e., partly a result of our physical constitution), ordinary people instinctively understood that there was some sort of connection. All information concerning human beings as living organisms is recorded in our genes. Is there any quality we possess, whether visible or invisible, that is not related to genetic factors? In the field of psychiatry, biological factors are receiving more attention even with regard to personality disorders. Who we are now is dependent upon both the tendencies with which we were born and the environment that has acted upon them.

As you may be aware, many of the genes we are born with remain dormant our entire lives. This means that although a given group of people may have a certain set of genes in common, the information contained in those genes will be expressed in some of those individuals and not in others. Current thinking about the genetic factors believed to be related to autism spectrum disorders is not based on the simplistic premise that the presence of a particular gene will automatically result in that individual having an ASD. There are a number of different genes involved, and it is believed that when these are switched on, expressed in a particular pattern due to some form of trigger, the result is an autism spectrum disorder. A large percentage of fathers and grandfathers of children on the spectrum are engineers, and it is thought that the same set of genes that can give rise to an ASD can also—when expressed in a certain pattern—give rise to superior skill in logical thinking and

mathematical ability (Baron-Cohen *et al.* 1997; Wheelwright and Baron-Cohen 2001).

People on the autism spectrum represent 1 percent of the population, and we can assume that many times this number have the same set of genes without actually having the disorder.

Many parents have told me that learning that their children had HFA or AS made them aware that they themselves also had the triad of impairments. Sometimes both parents have symptoms of the triad, but the manifestation may be different for each. For example, in terms of social characteristics, the father might be an introverted scholarly type, while the mother might be a tough, fearless person who has carved out a unique life. Such parents often lead rich and fulfilling lives precisely because of the triad; those who acknowledge these characteristics in themselves and work at using them to their advantage are often able to give their children realistic and effective support in a way that other parents cannot. Concerning the purpose of life, such people demonstrate by their own example that each individual can and should aim toward a life of fulfilment based on his or her own individual values. In my work as a doctor in clinical practice, it is parents like these who have taught me that the triad characteristics are not an illness, but rather a personality type that includes a number of strengths.

Lorna Wing, a British psychiatrist whose daughter had Kanner's Syndrome, has echoed Hans Asperger's observation that "great artists and scientists have to have some or all of the traits of this syndrome in order to concentrate on their chosen subject to the exclusion of all else, for at least some of the time" (from Wing's foreword to *Have you Heard of Asperger's Syndrome?* by Uchiyama 2002). When reading detailed, unembellished biographies, it is not unusual to find that the triad characteristics are the driving force behind the achievement of the dreams of people who are considered "great men" or "great women." If there is a possibility that you carry genetic factors related to the autism spectrum, this means that you also at the same time carry the genetic potential for greatness.

In addition, if one of your children is born with Kanner's Syndrome, the chances that the next child will also be born with it is thought to be only 5 percent—meaning that it is statistically much more likely that subsequent children will not have the disorder. Moreover, the percentage of children with Kanner's Syndrome born to families that have no prior cases of the disorder is overwhelmingly high. Thus, any one of us, regardless of family medical history, has the potential to have a child with an autism spectrum disorder.

As long as speaking about heredity remains taboo, misunderstandings about genetic factors will persist. Progress in research into the genetic factors related to ASDs may result in new breakthroughs in diagnosis and treatment. As a medical expert, it is my sincere hope that we will be liberated from the misconceptions that cause parents to feel their child's ASD is somehow their fault or that they have unfairly burdened the child's siblings.

IV. Disorders Similar to or Comorbid with ASDs

This section describes attention deficit hyperactivity disorder (ADHD) and learning disabilities or disorders (LDs), which can be difficult to distinguish from autism spectrum disorders or may appear in combination with them.

Attention Deficit Hyperactivity Disorder (ADHD)

Attention deficit hyperactivity disorder (ADHD) is the diagnostic term used by the American Psychiatric Association in its Diagnostic and Statistical Manual of Mental Disorders, fourth edition (DSM-IV; APA 1994) and is equivalent to the term hyperkinetic disorder as used by the World Health Organization (WHO 1992). It is also almost synonymous with the commonly used term hyperactivity syndrome.

To give you an idea of what ADHD actually is, I'll start by describing two elementary school children, Akio and Yuko.

The Different "Faces" of ADHD

Akio

Akio is in third grade. Since kindergarten, he has been notoriously unruly and has chalked up countless "daring" escapades. Although he no longer wanders around in the middle of class, his teacher is constantly telling him to "Zip your lip!" His desk drawer is always a mess, filled with crumpled handouts from who-knows-when. He frequently loses his pencils or erasers, but since everyone knows that Akio's pencils are the ones with the chewed-up ends, they always find their way back to his desk by the end of the school day even if he has forgotten to write his name on them. Oh, yes, and just this morning Akio lost his balance and crashed over backwards when he was rocking back and forth in his chair. The whole class erupted with laughter. Koichi, the boy who sits next to him, was pointing and laughing. Akio was so mad when he picked himself up from the floor that he knocked over Koichi's desk. And the teacher … When Akio came to his senses, the teacher was grasping him firmly by the shoulders, as usual, and saying, "Calm down! Calm down!"

By the fourth period, just before lunch, Akio had regained some composure. He began to think, "It's all Koichi's fault. He should never have laughed at me… Oh no. I've done it again. Nobody likes me… But who cares. I hate them all anyway. But… But I… I…"

Akio's mother dreads reading the notes he brings home from his teacher. "Oh dear," she always thinks, "what has he done this time? But he's so much better than he used to be. I wish my mother-in-law would stop telling me, 'If you don't discipline him better, Akio is going to suffer later in life.' It's me who's suffering!"

Yuko

Yuko is in second grade. Her teachers often remark that she is so quiet they tend to forget she's there. When the family went for a drive the other day, her parents loaded the car with her noisy brothers and didn't even realize that they had driven off without her. That shows not only how quiet she is but also what a quintessential dawdler and daydreamer she is. Although she tries to remind herself during every class that she must listen carefully to the teacher, the same sort of thing keeps happening: she might suddenly remember, for example, a TV program she was watching the night before on octopuses being born. As she sits pondering how nice it must feel to have eight legs and float through the water, a whole hour passes.

Today it is raining. Yuko is a slow walker. When she finally reaches school and then closes her umbrella, her classmate Junko looks at her in surprise and asks, "Where's your bookbag?" "Oh no," Yuko thinks, "What shall I do? I forgot my bookbag. I forgot it because I was using an umbrella." The moment she realizes this, her hands and feet go cold. "What's wrong with me?" she wonders. She is so sad she feels like crying.

Yuko's mother finds it difficult to fathom what goes on in her daughter's mind. When asked to write a composition or to solve difficult math word problems, the child appears to be reasonably able. But no matter how she is scolded, Yuko continues to make simple errors in writing, spelling, and arithmetic. When Yuko's mother sees her little girl's face pinched and pale with fear because she cannot find the notebook lying right in front of her, she worries that her daughter has some form of intellectual disability. At a recent parent-teacher meeting, she was shocked to learn that her daughter had forgotten her knapsack three times already since she entered second grade. She hopes Yuko's grandfather never finds out. If he does, he'll call her "chicken brain" again and say that like a chicken all she has to do is walk three paces and she forgets everything. She dreads hearing him say that. Thank goodness Yuko is human. She'd be the first to be eaten if she were an animal in the wild.

Akio and Yuko appear to be very different, yet both of these elementary school students may have ADHD.

What is ADHD?

ADHD is a condition diagnosed on the basis of three characteristics unrelated to the triad of impairments that defines the autism spectrum: inattention, hyperactivity, and impulsivity. To paraphrase the criteria defined in the DSM-IV (APA 1994), ADHD is diagnosed when the following conditions have been met:

★ Inattention, hyperactivity, and impulsivity are stronger than warranted by the child's developmental age (level of intellectual development).

★ Symptoms are not transitory. (They continue for six months or more.)

★ Symptoms appear before the age of seven.

★ Symptoms are not limited to just one setting such as school or the home.

★ Symptoms negatively affect the child's life.

★ Symptoms are not caused by some other disability or psychiatric disorder.

The symptoms of ADHD are broadly divided into two categories— attention deficit and hyperactivity-impulsivity—and there are three types of ADHD, defined by how the symptoms are exhibited: children with both attention deficit and hyperactivity-impulsivity will be diagnosed with the "combined" type (Akio may fall into this category); those whose overriding difficulty is with attentiveness will be diagnosed with the "predominately inattentive" type (Yuko may fall into this category); and those who exhibit mainly hyperactive-impulsive behavior will be diagnosed with the "hyperactive-impulsive" type.

Even more so than with autism spectrum disorders, ADHD tends to be blamed for the child's character or poor discipline. Yet the disorder is often accompanied by abnormalities in EEGs and is thought to result from an imbalance in development that is determined by some characteristic of the brain.

Parents and teachers who have trouble accepting the ADHD diagnosis frequently tell me, "But there have always been children like this." That is absolutely true. The prevalence of ADHD is estimated to range from 3 to 7 percent (1 out of every 15 to 35 people), and there have always been one or two children in every class who fit the description of this disorder. But it has also become increasingly clear that special supports can be very effective in managing this disorder.

Symptoms of ADHD

Let's examine the three broad symptom categories that constitute ADHD in more detail: inattention, hyperactivity, and impulsivity.

Inattention

The term "inattention" is often misinterpreted to mean that the child is constantly distracted and unable to concentrate on anything. A mother might conclude, for example, that her child can't possibly have an attention deficit disorder because he is able to concentrate on playing video games for hours. But there are many more facets to the issue of attention than this. Paradoxically, as discussed below, an unusually strong ability to concentrate on just one thing can actually be a sign of attention deficit and is an indication that the child should be examined more closely.

Inattention is evaluated on the basis of a person's social judgment concerning a task that he is not good at and does not really want to do, but knows that he should. This includes, for example, a child's attitude during a class he doesn't like or his response when asked to tidy up when he doesn't want to. Children who are inattentive tend to make a lot of careless mistakes, which become more conspicuous from about grade two or three, when classroom tests start to become more formal. Children may have problems with attention in a number of areas, such as:

★ *Difficulty focusing attention on a specific object*: This includes having one's attention drawn equally by, for example, the teacher, a nearby classmate's eraser, and noises coming from the hallway while a lesson is in progress. It also refers to general absentmindedness, a tendency to tune out when people are speaking, daydreaming, and so on.

★ *Difficulty using moderation when dividing ones' attention*: This includes completely forgetting what you have been doing as soon as your attention is directed at something new, or becoming totally oblivious to your surroundings when you see something you like—to the extent that you might consequently bump into things or step on them.

★ *Difficulty resisting distractions*: This includes being easily distracted by slight noises or movements, or, for example, reading a comic book found under the bed while cleaning your room and leaving the rest of the job unfinished.

These examples illustrate clearly why children with ADHD are able to concentrate with such great intensity on things that they like: it is precisely because they find it hard to divide or shift the focus of their attention once something has captured their interest. This explains the paradox introduced earlier, wherein unusually strong concentration can actually be a sign of ADHD.

Hyperactivity

Although it is easier to spot hyperactivity when it involves obvious "locomotion," so to speak—for example, an inability to stay seated, stand in line for any length of time, or refrain from constantly moving about—this type of conspicuous physical restlessness often subsides as the child grows older. From around the middle of elementary school, when typically developing children have more or less settled down, one can begin to notice hyperactive behavior that does not involve major body movements: the child might be able to remain in his chair, but one part of his body will always be moving. His legs will jiggle, for example, or perhaps he will fidget with his hands or chew on his pencil. He might rock back and forth in his chair until he falls over or be unable to stop talking during the lesson even when reprimanded.

Impulsivity

Children who are very impulsive do not hesitate before acting or expressing their emotions. Perhaps one way of describing this is that they are unable to store things up inside and assess them first. Impulsivity is frequently characterized by not being able to wait your turn or to wait for the teacher to call on you when you know the answer, or becoming so overexcited when playing that other children are put off.

Relationship between the Autism Spectrum and ADHD

International standards stipulate that children who have been diagnosed with a pervasive developmental disorder (PDD) should not be given an additional diagnosis of ADHD even when they exhibit all the symptoms of the disorder. (PDD is practically synonymous with ASD; for more on this, see page 31.) The thinking is that when inattention, hyperactivity, and impulsivity appear in children on the autism spectrum, those symptoms are caused by the ASD and a separate label is not warranted. In reality, however, there are children with Asperger's Syndrome who constantly make careless mistakes in arithmetic while fully understanding the meaning of the problems they are attempting to solve. An ADHD-like symptom of this particular nature cannot be adequately explained by the triad of impairments.

At the same time, it is known that children on the autism spectrum do have distinctive problems with the way they direct their attention, such as weak central coherence (see page 54). Research has not yet answered the question of whether or not the inattention seen in children diagnosed with ADHD (and not with autism spectrum disorders) is of the same nature as the inattention seen in those who are on the spectrum.

I believe that until this important puzzle is solved, it is best to set aside the assertion that an additional diagnosis of ADHD is unnecessary for children on the autism spectrum. By making a dual diagnosis of both ADHD and ASD when symptoms point in both directions, we can ensure that children do not fall through the cracks and are considered eligible for any and all relevant interventions. For advice concerning how to treat children on the spectrum who exhibit ADHD symptoms, please refer to Uchiyama,

Mizuno and Yoshida 2002. In addition, measures for hyperactivity that can be taken in early childhood are explained on page 171.

Learning Disabilities and Disorders (LDs)

There are two separate terms that are referred to as LDs, each of which has a different definition: learning disorders (a term preferred by the American Psychiatric Association) and learning disabilities (preferred by the National Joint Committee on Learning Disabilities). There are also experts who use the term LD in still a different way that is not covered by either of the two standard definitions.

Different Uses of the Term LD

It is important to be aware of differences in the usage of the term LD, and therefore I have explained them in detail below.

LD Confined to Reading, Writing, and Arithmetic

In Japanese we have the age-old reference to "reading, writing, and abacus." So, too, the English language refers to the "three Rs": reading, writing, and (a)rithmetic. Narrowly defined, LD—and here the term learning disorders is signified—means a handicap in one or more of these three areas of skill that is incommensurate with the person's IQ.

Many Japanese child psychiatrists use this definition in making a diagnosis partly because it is advocated by the American Psychiatric Association. Naturally, this concept does not have any relevance to very young children who are not yet at an age where ability in the three Rs is expected, and so the term LD in the sense of "learning disorder" is not applied to children in this age group.

Disabilities in Listening, Speaking, and Reasoning in Addition to the Three Rs

The National Joint Committee on Learning Disabilities uses LD—in this case, learning disabilities and not learning disorders—to signify a handicap in hearing, speaking, and/or reasoning that is incommensurate with a person's IQ, in addition to a similar handicap involving reading, writing, and/or arithmetic. This is the sense in which LD was used in a 1999 report to the Ministry of Education. When this ministry later became the Ministry of Education, Culture, Sports, Science and Technology, the same definition was adopted. As a result, the term LD as used in the field of education is different from the term as used by child psychiatrists.

Still Other Variants of the Term LD

Some experts individually adopt the perspective that LD includes cases in which socialization is much less developed than warranted by the individual's level of intellectual ability. Both this conception and the use of the term "nonverbal LD" exist independently of the two standard definitions discussed above.

The Case for Limiting the Term LD to Handicaps Involving the Three Rs

Is there such a thing as a child who has impairments in reasoning ability (social imagination) or social development but does not have the entire triad of impairments? All the child psychiatrists I have ever come in contact with are unanimous in saying that they have never encountered such a child, and, indeed, neither have I. The children we treat invariably exhibit all three impairments as a set. Because there exists a vast store of ideas on how to support children

with autism spectrum disorders—that is, those who have the triad of impairments—overlooking the existence of an ASD because of a too-broad definition of LD turns out to be highly disadvantageous to the child being examined and treated.

Once a child's condition has been explained by the term LD, parents and experts may neglect to reassess the child's difficulties from the alternative perspective of the autism spectrum. This is similar to the problem wherein diagnoses of ADHD or LD (based on difficulty with the three Rs) are ruled out once a child is found to be on the spectrum. Even though we know that this is not right, experts like myself tend to see children only through the lens of our own field of specialization. This is why it is important to be very specific in any given assessment in establishing exactly what has been looked at. To do so, I personally believe that it is better to restrict the definition of LD to the three Rs.

Relationship between the Autism Spectrum and LDs

The DSM-III-R (APA 1987), the revised third edition of the American Psychiatric Association's book of diagnostic criteria, disallowed the dual diagnosis of PDD and LD; thus, for example, a child with PDD who also had a writing disability would be diagnosed only as having PDD. This was changed in the fourth edition, the DSM-IV (APA 1994), so that a twin finding of both disorders is now allowed.

In reality, it is not unusual for children on the high-functioning end of the autism spectrum to also have an LD. Among the many children I have met, the combination of Asperger's Syndrome with a writing disability is quite common, followed by combination with a math disability. As for reading, although there are of course a great many children on the spectrum who are not good at comprehending the meaning of what they read (this is sometimes included under reading disabilities), these cases are explained by the triad of impairments, and therefore I do not make an additional diagnosis of LD.

Chapter 2

Rethinking Your Parenting Style

Putting Your Knowledge of the Autism Spectrum to Work

I. Nurturing Communication Skills

The Objectives of Intervention

Progress in development during early childhood is closely linked to stability in daily life. To some people, promoting development may conjure up an image of sitting a child down at a desk to study, but this is a misconception. At this age, "development" entails acquiring appropriate life skills and learning to use them more and more reliably. Supports that help achieve this are what we mean when we talk about "interventions." It is a terrible waste when parents, blinded by the narrow image of "studying," miss the point, or else give up entirely on the idea of intervening from a belief that they do not have enough time or energy. If parents are bending the rules that govern daily life in order to coax their children to sit at their desks each day, they are approaching the problem from the wrong direction and the chief result will inevitably be mutual exasperation and exhaustion. This kind of life is far removed from genuine therapeutic intervention.

It is important to introduce the perspective of daily intervention early in parenting your child. Actually, in most cases the very interventions that make life easier for both parent and child, especially those that form bridges onto the next leg of development, are just what the child needs. In contrast, anything that continues to create more and more work and to make life more difficult is unlikely to be helpful for your child. This is true even if the intervention is based on the advice of an "expert."

The long-term objective of intervention is to help children grow into adults who have self-confidence and take pride in their achievements. If force-feeding a child a skill results in a loss of confidence and self-esteem, in the end you achieve nothing. Intervention is not a form of ascetic training in which the present must be sacrificed for some unspecified time in the future. The most important factor in raising children to become confident and proud adults is giving them as much confidence and security as possible in early childhood. You teach them skills because it is certainly more helpful to this end to have skills than to be deprived of them. But if you do not constantly keep straight in your mind the difference between the end—the long-term objective—and the means—the techniques used to achieve this purpose—your interventions will be ineffective, despite your best intentions.

Each child is different. Even if they are the same age and gender and have the same diagnosis, no two children are identical. The amount of time and emotional reserves a mother has will also vary greatly from one home to another. For optimum results, a unique at-home plan should be worked out for each child based on his or her individual characteristics and family circumstances. In fact, however, in many locations such individualized assessments are not available. And in some cases, the mother herself hesitates to go for an assessment. In this chapter, I will explain some of the techniques and approaches that are considered effective for many children on the autism spectrum. Unfortunately, however, there is no advice that will fit absolutely every child. If you try an intervention in your home for three months and still find that your life has not become easier in any way and that raising your child has not become more enjoyable, then please feel free to consider discarding that intervention and moving on. If possible, consult an expert for advice.

A better parent is not one who makes a greater sacrifice. Can this child you are raising really grow up to become a confident adult if you never even crack a smile? Interventions should not require either you or your child to grit your teeth here and now with the goal of smiling in the future. Rather they should allow you to seize the present, this precious time in your lives that only comes once, and live in it fully, with greater convenience and more joy.

Developing Communication Skills

Impairments in communication are a basic symptom common to all children on the autism spectrum. Parents often ask me how they can help expand their children's expressive language skills.

First, it is important not to set developmental targets that focus solely on increasing vocabulary or on speaking longer sentences. Remember that one characteristic symptom of ASDs is qualitative impairment of communication; for children with this type of impairment, progress in the narrow sense of acquiring more words and grammar is not necessarily reflected in actual communication ability. In some cases, overzealous teaching of vocabulary can actually be counterproductive and hinder the acquisition of usable communication skills.

The key to developing these skills is making children aware as early as possible that exchanging information with other people is convenient, fun, and necessary. This foundation is extremely shaky for children on the spectrum, whether or not they have speech, and must be strengthened in order to get development on track during the preschool period and to aid learning and emotional stability once the child enters school.

Given the importance of helping children develop reliable, usable skills at an early age, we should not be overly particular about the

form of communication. In fact, as a general rule, children will find it easier to experience the convenience and joy of communicating if you use forms other than expressive language.

When I make this recommendation, many parents respond with, "But if I use other methods, won't my child stop speaking at all?" or "Why should I go to the trouble of teaching my child other communication methods when he (she) can already speak?" My answer is that it is easier to whet children's appetites for communication by helping them to accumulate successes with gestures or cards than by forcing them to convey their wishes and understand yours verbally when this strategy only works for them sometimes. An early grasp of the meaning of communication (convenience, enjoyment, necessity) aids the acquisition of new vocabulary.

Developing Receptive Language Skills

Communication can be divided into expression (transmitting information) and reception (receiving information). Most parents who are concerned about delayed language development focus their worries on expression, perhaps because the presence or absence of speech is so obvious, whereas problems with comprehension are not so easily identified or evaluated. Be that as it may, the development of proper expression depends upon proper reception, and I will begin with the latter precisely because it is so often overlooked.

Easy Tosses for Beginners

Communication is like playing catch. If the person you are playing with (your child) is a beginner, you should throw the ball in a way that makes it easy for him or her to catch it. As the child accumulates experience at successfully catching the ball, he will come to understand the convenience and joy of communication. If every toss is too difficult to catch, it is only natural that the child will come to dislike the game. If your child constantly misses or fumbles the ball and wants to give up, it is time to reflect upon your own lack of skill in throwing.

Occasionally I meet parents and kindergarten teachers who announce that, "This child will have to function in a regular classroom once he goes to school, and therefore even if it is a little difficult for him, and even if all he can do is watch others and then imitate their behavior, I expect him to do his best to keep up with instructions that match his age level." The stakes involved in such a gamble, however, are too high. The agony children must go through in order to regain their motivation or confidence once they have lost it is indescribable. You as a parent or teacher will also lose your motivation.

Accurately Determining your Child's Language Comprehension Level

In order to help your child improve his receptive communication ability, you must first determine what he can currently comprehend. How many words and how much content can he understand when communication comes in the form of pure speech—that is, without dependence on visual clues or familiar patterns? Does he remember vocabulary in a unique order compared with other children? Does he tend to give words his own peculiar meaning? What about words that express concepts or verbs? Can he still understand a given word when it is used by a different person or in a different situation? Can he bring you back two things that you do not usually ask for as a pair? Can he perform two unrelated tasks that you assign in a single set of instructions? Can he use grammatical particles in distinguishing between the subject and the object of a sentence in order to understand its meaning?

All these questions are not meant to make you feel defensive, but rather to illustrate that it is very difficult to assess the comprehension of children on the autism spectrum when they are in a routine setting full of clues and familiar patterns. Parents watching their children undergo IQ tests in the clinic often exclaim, "But he knows the answer to that question!" or "He would have been able to answer if you had asked him like this..." I am not saying that I do not believe these parents. But a child's behavior in a test situation is also one reality. Identifying the gap between performance in a test situation and under everyday circumstances and then considering the causes is very important in understanding a child's qualitative problems in language comprehension.

In typical development, children generally can use roughly 90 to 95 percent of the words that they can comprehend. They can also understand when any of the words they can use are spoken to them. This is not true, however, for children on the autism spectrum. These youngsters may use long sentences or words that express concepts, for example, of number, size, or time (e.g., "Can you buy three big pieces of cake tomorrow, Mom?"), but this does not necessarily mean that they actually understand the meaning of all the words. Because of this type of verbal precocity, the comprehension of children on the high-functioning end of the autism spectrum is often mistakenly evaluated as being greater than it really is, resulting in unrealistic expectations.

The Ability to Comprehend Other Communication Methods is Not Uniform

Another problematic misunderstanding is that "all children on the autism spectrum can understand word or picture cards." It is certainly true that visual communication cues are easier for such children to grasp than the spoken word, which vanishes instantly and does not allow ample time for meaning to be confirmed. Many two- to three-year-olds on the autism spectrum who also have intellectual disabilities, however, are not yet capable of understanding that two-dimensional information such as pictures or photographs can represent either three-dimensional objects or things that are not concrete, such as situations or activities. In such cases, it is more effective to communicate information by using actual objects, such as by holding up their school bag in order to convey that it is time to go to kindergarten or by showing them the back brush to tell them that it is time to have a bath. Depending on the degree of intellectual disability, even this might not be understood, in which case it might be necessary to use physical contact such as taking them by the hand or putting your hand on their shoulder to indicate that it is time for a transition to another activity.

Using Strengths to Encourage Language Development

At one time, parents of children who have delayed language development were urged to talk to their children as much as possible. This approach, however, does not work for children on the autism spectrum. It is more effective to use simple language accompanied by visual information to convey your meaning.

Let's suppose, for example, that a child does not know the meaning of the word "orange." If you say "orange" every time you give your child one, he will begin to think, "my mother says 'orange' whenever I see this food with this particular taste, shape, and colour." In other words, the visible object (meaning) and the sound (word) become paired, and the child is thus able to acquire the word "orange." This method of teaching utilizes the tendency of children on the autism spectrum to be good at visual observation and at forming pairs.

But what would happen if you spoke like this: "Look. Here's an orange. It's good, isn't it? Eat lots. Your grandmother in Shizuoka sent them. Wasn't that nice? Grandma is really kind, isn't she? Let's go visit her again when we can." Children on the autism spectrum cannot glean from this monologue the sound that goes with the object in front of them. There is a danger that they might mistakenly associate the object with, for example, the word "Shizuoka" and say "Eat Shizuoka" when they want an orange. As children on the autism spectrum find it very difficult to change conclusions they've already reached, it will be very hard to correct such an association once they have made it.

Long, incomprehensible explanations will not promote better language comprehension. Instead, show the object and add simple words. Avoiding adding words that the child can't understand is also very important.

In addition to making it easier for children to understand the meaning of a word, this method has another advantage. A child who is always addressed with words that he or she can comprehend will one day realize that the sounds people make all have a particular meaning. This will in turn lead to the realization that people are not just throwing noises at one another but that they are exchanging meaning. This is the basis for verbal language development, and it may be precisely what is lacking in children who speak incomprehensible "jargon." Rather than rejoicing or despairing over the number of words a child can say, it is wiser to concentrate on helping him or her develop such a foundation.

If you practice this approach, you will find that you no longer talk about things that you can't show, and your instructions will become more concrete. Instead of saying, "Wait a minute," you'll learn to say, "Look at this book" (with the result that the child is able to wait). Rather than saying, "Stop wandering around," you might put your hand on a chair and say, "Sit here."

This method of "show and tell" instruction is not only easier for your child to understand, but also gives you more opportunity to offer praise. It is much easier to praise a child who complies with your positive instruction to "Sit here" than it is to praise a child who complies in some way with a negative command such as "Stop wandering around!"

Communication ability varies widely, even for children on the autism spectrum who are the same age, and some children do want a logical explanation. Even so, limiting what you say to what the child can understand and using visual aids to promote understanding and acceptance should still be the common principles in teaching communication.

The Danger of Not Providing Comprehensible Input

I often see children on the autism spectrum, both kindergarteners and elementary school students, who follow along after everyone else or are taken by the hand and led by a teacher or classmate because they do not respond to verbal prompts given to the entire class, such as the instruction that it's time to change classrooms. Is this strategy developmentally appropriate? I believe that this type of situation is extremely unfortunate if the child is one who could understand, for example, that it is time to go home when shown

the uniform hat worn outdoors or a picture of the kindergarten bus. It represents the loss of valuable opportunities for practicing linguistic reception. This type of situation is also dangerous. Even if the child gets on the bus, this "successful" outcome will not develop his or her confidence. Instead, he or she will most certainly be filled with anxiety. Surrounded by information they cannot understand, some children begin to reject all information, even that which they have the potential to comprehend. In addition, such situations can cause children who are beginning to become aware of failure and success to lose confidence and make them timid or, conversely, frustrated and short-tempered. They can also trigger reluctance to go to kindergarten or school and aggravate tics or hair loss. (Tics are thought to be related to brain type and hair loss to abnormalities in the immune system, but both conditions are aggravated by stress.)

In short, you must not assume that as long as the child performs the hoped-for action, that it is adequate to provide only the minimum of instruction. The most important thing is for the child to perform the action independently and with confidence. Preparing information that matches the child's level of development is essential for his or her emotional stability.

Comprehension is Variable

Even when information is provided in an appropriate format for comprehension, there will be times when a child can understand it and times when he or she cannot. Although this is true in typical development as well, in children on the autism spectrum the differences are more extreme, and this is one factor that makes it difficult to accurately assess their ability to understand language. Large variations in communication ability depending on such factors as the individual's state of health, level of anxiety or tension, and so on is one diagnostic indicator of an autism spectrum disorder.

Parents are only human, and there may be times when you exclaim, "You know what I mean!" or "Stop fooling around!" But you know better than anyone else that such admonitions will not help correct your child's behavior. For children with auditory hypersensitivity, the mere sound of a critical voice is a distressing stimulus that will make them want to shut their parent out. Similarly, a barrage of instructions will only serve to make your child feel more confused.

Children on the autism spectrum find it difficult to judge which "transmitter," that is, which person speaking, they are supposed to pay attention to in a given situation. Moreover, when their minds become preoccupied with something that has captured their attention or interest, they become oblivious to any other information, whether visual or auditory. If you want them to focus on you, you must first remove extraneous stimuli (things they can see and hear) and only then call their attention. (See page 172 for information on how to eliminate extraneous stimuli.)

Another method when you cannot get through is to present the information once again in a form that is easier for the child to comprehend. For example, if your child usually understands when you say, "clean-up time," but today the words do not seem to penetrate because of fatigue, try putting the toy box down right in front of him or her as you voice your invitation to clean up.

Remember that the level of information that can be processed can easily change owing to such factors as distractions (both internal—i.e., mental—and external), anxiety, tension, or changes in physical health or level of energy.

Enjoying Receptive Communication

Communication ability develops as the individual experiences the convenience of being able to exchange information. If your child has realized the merits of conveying information but has not yet picked up on the advantages of receptive communication, start practicing by presenting information he or she will enjoy receiving. Once again, you are more likely to see results if you utilize your child's strengths (making visual observations and forming pairs, or associations) by, for example, holding up his or her school bag when you say "Time to go."

Once your child realizes the convenience or necessity of receiving information, you can take this one step further and begin teaching the joy of receiving information through play activities with adults. Most parenting guides recommend reading picture books aloud to children who are slow to begin speaking, but in the case of youngsters on the autism spectrum this will only help development for the few who have a very high level of language comprehension. Instead try starting with playtime activities that conform to set patterns and focus primarily on visual information. For example, action songs are a type of game that all children, from those who have marked intellectual disabilities to those who are high functioning, can enjoy provided that the song and manner of participation are selected to suit the individual.

"*Sakana ga haneta*" (The Fish Jumped) and "*Hige jiisan*" (The Bearded Grandfather) are popular action songs with children on the autism spectrum.[1] Perhaps it is the clear movements, abundant repetition, and unique intonation that appeal. With action songs,

---

1   These songs are similar to the English children's songs "Itsy Bitsy Spider" and "Heads, Shoulders, Knees and Toes."

it is possible to incorporate many different activities to achieve a broad range of developmental goals in fun ways that suit the age or situation of particular children. Depending on the child, possible ways of participating might include enjoying just watching, and perhaps mimicking afterwards; mimicking on the spot; using eye contact to communicate a sense of enjoyment; using words or cards as a way of asking to do it again; choosing which songs or activities to do that day by using cards; or participating in some sort of beginning and ending ritual (such as a special greeting and farewell) to mark the transition into and out of the activity. The make-believe play activities described on page 149 as therapies for impairment of social imagination can be used in this way, too. Although these types of play lend themselves easily to adaptation and the incorporation of different goals, be careful not to keep changing how you play a particular game. Children on the autism spectrum are reassured by patterns; in fact, they excel at enjoying patterns. Remember to utilize this strength in order to develop their weaker skills in receptive communication.

Other easy-to-enjoy activities for developing receptive communication include using a felt board to tell stories with plenty of repetition (see the illustration on page 119) and using homemade stick puppets to engage in simple, fixed dialogues. You can add these activities gradually to suit the child's current level of development. Of course, if the child seems to enjoy it, reading picture books aloud is perfectly fine. Trying this may even provide an opportunity for the child to discover a new form of enjoyment. But if your child gazes out of the window at passing cars or is otherwise distracted despite your enthusiastic storytelling, it is a sign that this activity should be saved for some time in the future.

Felt Board Storytelling

When your Child Cannot Accept Instructions to Stop

Although not responding when told to stop doing something may appear to be a problem with receptive communication, it is also related to impaired social imagination and socialization and is greatly influenced by problems in expressive communication. I will address this issue from each of these perspectives.

Naturally, understanding and accepting are two different things. Even if your instructions are developmentally appropriate, taking into account the characteristics of autistic children in general and your own child in particular, this will not make toeing the line any more pleasant if the line itself is abhorrent. It is important to guess the child's level of intolerance with reference to autistic characteristics. For example, if someone said to me, "Let me press these hot tongs against your hand," I would not like it no matter how gently or persuasively he asked. Likewise for a child who is hypersensitive to sound, there are some requests that are simply unreasonable, such as telling him that he must not panic and run away when he hears the starting gun at the school Sports Day. Situations related to this topic are also explained on page 182 in response to a question concerning hypersensitivity to sound, and on page 136 in the section on providing supports for impairment of social imagination.

Here, let's consider the difficulty of accepting a command to stop from the perspective of receptive communication.

First, consider whether your child really understood the instruction you gave. Even children on the high-functioning end of the autism spectrum cannot decipher meanings that are implied, rather than explicitly stated in words. Take for example the child who, when his mother exclaims in exasperation, "How many times do I have to tell you?!" responds with "Um, five times?" Or the child who, when told by her teacher, "No five-year-old would do such a thing!" walks over and joins the four-year-old kindergarten class. Or another child who, when his teacher says, "You are annoying your friends," continues what he is doing without realizing that she wants him to stop. All of these examples are a result of inappropriate instructions that do not match the child's receptive language abilities. To take a slightly more extreme case, a child at an even more limited developmental level may not realize that "You mustn't stand up!" means "Sit down" and may not be able to comprehend specifically what is meant by the abstract term, "No!" Keep your instructions clear and concrete and make sure they match the receptive capability of the child.

Confusion is often part and parcel of a situation where something is being forbidden. And when confusion reigns, signals that a child would usually understand may not even be registering. It is better in such cases to avoid long, involved attempts at persuasion and instead get your message across in a visual manner that is even more simple and concise than you would usually use.

Developing Expressive Language Skills

Parents and teachers tend to think, "If only he could say more words or longer sentences." But some children may lack the desire to communicate to others, even though they spend much time talking to themselves. If they are not choosing their words purposefully, with the intention of bringing about a specific reaction or outcome as a result of what they say, then it is difficult to call their speech communication in the real sense. Also, even if they chatter fluently about things that interest them, if they cannot communicate to others that they are having difficulty and ask for appropriate help, then their ability to use communication for practical convenience must be considered weak.

Communicating Problems and Asking for Help

Even among children on the autism spectrum who talk a lot, it is surprisingly rare to find those who can verbally convey the fact that they don't understand and ask someone to explain. Furthermore, their families often do not see this as a serious problem.

How does your child express his or her difficulties and ask for help? It is not unusual for children with ASDs to convey a lack of comprehension through such behaviors as wandering aimlessly away with a silly grin on their faces, parroting, suddenly launching into a spiel on their favorite topic, or responding with something that does not answer the question. At times like this, we should ask ourselves whether we have given them enough clues or whether our question was too difficult. It is also necessary to actively teach them how to tell people that they do not understand.

When a child on the spectrum wants help, often he or she will try to get others to notice by announcing the difficulty to no one in particular, saying, for example, "Oh, this lid is tight" or by pressing an object wordlessly into someone's hands. If these actions fail to bring assistance, the child may give up or fly into a tantrum.

The easiest way to get a message across to another person is to make a direct appeal. Neurotypical children will attract someone's

attention by calling to them, by using eye contact, or by some form of body language and then, while appealing to the other's desire to help, will explain that they are in trouble and ask for assistance. Children on the autism spectrum cannot be expected to include all of these subtle nuances in their communication repertoire, and therefore it is more practical to teach them skills that will enable them to communicate more easily to others.

For high-functioning children who can understand the meaning of written words (from upper kindergarten through elementary school age) one common method is to place prompt cards for trouble situations where the children can see them. These cards, which say, "Please teach me," "I don't understand," or "I want to rest," are also called "reminders." They remind the children that there are ways they can ask for help or express problems. They also provide a script of what to say in such situations. The cards reassure the children that it is all right to say, "I don't understand" and help give them the courage to do so. Some children may need to give the card to the other person, while others may be able to say the words themselves as long as they have the card. It is also, of course, possible to use cards that do not rely on words. In some cases, a child can be instructed to go to the teacher (or to a designated "trouble-shooter" identified by a ribbon or other badge) and touch his or her sleeve when in trouble. A surprisingly large number of children on the autism spectrum simply are not aware that asking for help is one way of solving a problem, or else they lack the confidence to do so. The use of reminders as a means of encouraging them to convey necessary information is certainly worth a try.

Please Teach Me

Depending on the intellectual or chronological age of a child, there are cases where whining, becoming engrossed in perseverative behaviors, parroting, or fidgeting and making grunting sounds may be the most appropriate methods of expression they are currently capable of. There are periods during which we should accept handing someone an object or shoving an object at him or her as an acceptable way to ask for help. By demanding that the child perform at a higher level than he or she is able to, we risk nipping beginning attempts to ask for help in the bud, despite the fact that the techniques being used are appropriate to the child's current level of development. Such demands may also aggravate tantrums. A proper grasp of the child's developmental level is important, because the target level of expressive communication to aim for will differ in each case.

"I Don't Understand," "Please Help Me," and "I Want to Rest"

Teaching these three expressions early on may strike some as likely to encourage laziness or a tendency to not try, but in fact the opposite is true. "When I am in trouble, I can get help. When I get help, I can learn how to do things by myself. And learning to do something I couldn't do before makes me feel happy." Children who have not repeatedly experienced this sequence of outcomes are more likely to give up as soon as they think they might fail. Or they may be unable to let themselves off the hook unless they can complete the task and in the end are thrown into a panic, feeling exhausted or frustrated even when they do finish. Children on the autism spectrum find it difficult to recognize their own level of fatigue and to take breaks at appropriate intervals until they complete a task. They are also poor at judging whether a task is within their capacity and at drawing up a plan towards completion. Developing the ability to say, "I don't understand," "Please help me," or "I want to rest" is a very complex endeavour that involves not only communication but also many other interrelated issues fundamental to the autism spectrum. If children with ASDs are not explicitly taught this skill, they will pass through early childhood, elementary school, and adolescence and then into adulthood without the ability to express these things. It is quite possible that after finding employment they will work to the utmost limit of their endurance and then panic, abruptly quitting their jobs or suddenly exhibiting signs of psychological complications because, unnoticed, they have been driven into a corner. This type of problem can be experienced by any adult on the autism spectrum, from those who are severely intellectually disabled to those who are high functioning.

If a child communicates difficulty understanding or the need to rest so often that it interferes with life at home or at kindergarten, this is not a problem of expressive language. I suggest that in such cases you ask yourself whether the daily tasks set for him or her might be too difficult. Has the child been given the necessary information needed to see how and at what point the task will end? Could it be that you are now paying the price for demanding that your child strive to meet unrealistic goals? I suggest that rather than clamping down on protests of "I don't understand" or "I want to rest," you should be spurred by such protests to try setting more attainable goals and adjusting the environment so that he or she can meet your expectations without complaint.

Is it Possible to Teach Reciprocal Communication?

Enjoyment of reciprocal conversation in early childhood is a difficult goal even for high-functioning children on the autism spectrum. Having a reciprocal conversation means choosing a topic that is appropriate and mutually agreeable, supplying necessary information, enjoying the other person's reaction, savoring the information and emotions contained in that person's statements, and building on all of that when responding with your own statements. When described in this way, you may wonder if such a complicated act is possible for children at all, but neurotypical children enjoy reciprocal conversation by the time they are about five to six years old. Even three- or four-year-olds can enjoy reasonably reciprocal conversations when they are talking to adults:

> "But our child loves conversation so much that the first doctor we took him to said he wasn't autistic."

> "After he says something, he is very concerned about whether or not the other person makes a response, so I think he must be genuinely taking in what other people say. "

There are indeed children with autism whose love of conversation makes one want to argue like this. But if we examine them closely, they are really looking for a completely obedient audience. Or a prop in a one-man play, meant only to behave as the script calls for. Please forgive my bluntness, but this is not "conversation." It is a very elaborate form of talking to oneself, and this distinction must be understood very clearly. Some people erroneously believe that the emergence of this kind of behavior represents an improvement in reciprocity and that conversational and other social skills will automatically evolve even further with experience once the child enters a mainstream elementary school classroom. While it is possible to teach ways of exchanging information that will help avoid misunderstandings and communication methods that will not upset the listener (conversational rules), we cannot teach the feeling of communicating with someone on the same wavelength or the pleasure to be found in reciprocity itself.

In reality, there are children with Asperger's Syndrome (usually those who are at least in the third grade of elementary school) who can carry on conversations that seem quite reciprocal. But please consider and appreciate how difficult this must be and what an enormous achievement it truly is. They do not speak until the other person has stopped talking, and they listen carefully to what the person is saying, as if solving a riddle, in order to identify the facts contained in their statements and, ideally, to spot items that they can respond to. If so, they silently congratulate themselves, and if not, they may decide it's better to try Plan B. In this case, they switch topics, making sure to begin by saying, "This is changing the subject, but…" If the other person turns away or suddenly begins talking to someone else, they know that they have failed. Children who have shared these secrets with me have almost invariably concluded with, "That's why talking with friends is so exhausting." Here are still other strategies that have been described to me: "When I say what I'm really thinking, for some reason something bad always happens, so I usually make a habit of only saying the second thing that comes to mind." "At school I only talk when someone asks me a question." "During breaks, I pretend that I'm engrossed in reading a book." "I only talk to A." My heart aches when pondering these independently devised techniques in the art of conversational self-defense.

Given a chance to talk about what they like, for example, railroads, these youngsters could exchange information for hours. To the casual observer, the conversations of children who both (or all) have ASDs may appear to fly off on one tangent after another, but afterwards the children themselves will exclaim, "It was so much fun talking together!" The type of interaction we think of as reciprocity is simply not native to their culture. Yet, in order to make life easier for us and for them, they master skills that help them adapt to our ways. We should first of all honour and respect their consideration and effort. Only then should we begin considering how much "reciprocity" it is reasonable to expect of a certain child at a particular time.

Enjoying the Rules of the Conversation "Game"

Children on the autism spectrum often do not realize that conversations have rules, but we can help them to experience this fact and enjoy following along. The special education pullout classes (resource rooms) at Japanese elementary schools skillfully weave into their programs activities that help children learn verbal patterns with specific rules. It is also possible to adopt this approach at home by introducing entertaining games. Of course, such activities must be developmentally appropriate if they are to work for a particular child. One way to tell whether an activity is appropriate is if both the parent and child enjoy it.

Three Clues, Charades, and Show and Tell are activities that can be adapted for enjoyment by children from the older kindergarten years and on through elementary school. Each of these games follows a clearly defined procedure that lets children have fun using expressive and receptive language governed by rules.

Three Clues is a quiz game in which one person has to guess what object the other person is thinking of based on three clues. For young children, it is best to let them choose one of several objects you have prepared well in advance so they have plenty of time to think of their hints while looking at the object. Even neurotypical children are not able to think of quiz questions that lead to a single answer—without actually giving the answer away—until they reach about age five; therefore, among children with ASDs this game as it is usually played is only appropriate for the very small number who are high functioning enough to participate. Adaptations can be made so that the game is easier to enjoy. For example, prepare a set of cards ahead of time with clues such as, "It's a fruit," "It's a piece of clothing," "You use it when you eat," "It's red," "It's round," and so on. Also prepare three frames by drawing them on a magnetic write and wipe board. Allow the child to convey his or her clues by selecting three cards and placing each one in a frame. By the time high-functioning children are in grade three or four, they will probably be able to make quiz questions concerning objects that they picture in their minds.

Charades, a game played by using gestures to represent an object (usually selected by drawing lots), is a surprisingly difficult task for children on the autism spectrum. Even those children who can communicate through gestures may focus on such a unique property of the object that those of us without ASDs find it hard to guess the answer. When miming a butterfly, they may focus on the long antennae, or, for a camera, the round lens. Interestingly, when children with ASDs play Charades together, they often understand each other's gestures immediately and guess the right answer. At such times, I am struck by the fact that the differences between our characteristics and theirs are cultural and cannot be judged as either better or worse.

For Show and Tell, one person stands in front of the group with a favorite object, talks about it, and asks and answers questions. Providing clear visual clues will make this activity go smoother. For example, you can distinguish between the speaker and the listeners by identifying where each should sit or stand, or by using a toy microphone for the speaker. The order in which children are to make their presentations can be shown by putting up photographs of each speaker on a board or by using number cards.

The important thing is to consistently conduct these kinds of activities at a level of challenge that is enjoyable for your child at each particular stage of development. If you establish a regular "game time," such as after snack time every day or after breakfast on Sundays, it can be a lot of fun. This type of routine provides a good opportunity for parents to leisurely assess the extent of visual supports their child needs, and it also makes it easier to maintain a balance between playing alone and playing with others. Above all, make it fun. In the home, where it is difficult to assess your child as a professional would, your child's degree of enjoyment can be your best measure of an activity's effectiveness. Be careful not to push an activity on your child. If he or she does not seem to be enjoying it much after one or two sessions, drop it and do something that you know will make both of you happy.

Show and Tell

Be Careful when Correcting Children's Verbal Mistakes

Even if two children are both on the high-functioning end of the autism spectrum, the expressive language issues that need addressing will differ with each. Specific advice is given on the basis of individual assessment. Although it is advantageous for children to receive professional language instruction with such aims as making their vocabularies larger and more well rounded and teaching them correct grammar, this kind of expert help is not always available; in these cases, it is risky for parents to try to instruct their children themselves. It is almost impossible to cultivate a sense of joy in communicating and avoid creating tension and distance in the parent-child relationship while correcting the child's grammatical and lexical errors. If you cannot have all three, then I unhesitatingly recommend that you give priority to the first two.

It is safer to confine corrections to modelling proper usage when opportunities present themselves naturally. For example, to correct the statement, "The duck is swimming on the pond" you can respond with, "Yes, the duck is swimming in the pond." If you were travelling in a foreign country and trying very hard to communicate despite your shaky command of the local language, wouldn't you resent someone who pointed out each of your pronunciation errors, one after the other? Wouldn't you feel like saying, "Stop picking on me! All I need are ten more years and my pronunciation will be just fine, thank you very much!"? The most important thing in communication is sharing the content conveyed. If you give priority to instructing rather than to enjoying the substance together, you may destroy your child's budding desire to communicate.

As far as conversations at home are concerned, just enjoy. As long as the meaning is communicated, that is enough.

During preschool and early elementary school, the conversation of neurotypical children also tends to switch erratically from one topic to another, so it is easy for parents of children with ASDs to think, "My child only needs to get a little more experience and practice." But those children are just revving up for take off. Once they have taxied down the runway and mastered the basics of understanding each other's verbally expressed emotions, their conversational and group activity skills will take flight; this high-altitude journey can be expected to occur throughout the middle and upper elementary school years (from grades three through six).

The erroneous belief by parents that success is just out of reach and only a few short steps away is one reason why many tend to seek a once-and-for-all "cure" for their children's expressive language difficulties—some sort of "fix" that will help their children appear "natural" or "normal." But we must be very cautious when assessing how much skill it is possible for a given child with an autism spectrum disorder to acquire through practice. And even before that, we must carefully assess whether such training will really contribute to that child's confidence, self-esteem, and *joie de vivre*.

Early Intervention for Inappropriate Approaches to Strangers

Inappropriate communication, such as talking to strangers, requires early intervention. When a child who has previously shown no interest in other people suddenly begins to approach total strangers in a one-sided fashion, parents and teachers often welcome this behavior wholeheartedly as a sign of "development." And the stranger thus approached will generally smile at this rare sight of simple childish innocence. But this is true only while the child is young.

If such interactions become more frequent without the child coming to realize that others have their own feelings and business of their own to attend to, he or she will run into problems in the future. When they reach the age at which others may begin to reject them, children on the high-functioning end of the autism spectrum tend to feel surprised and hurt, and some will attempt to change on their own. But often these efforts are unsuccessful. Thus, there is a danger that inappropriate interactions will result in rejection by peers, and when these older children reach adulthood their social approaches may be considered frightening or even interpreted as criminal behavior. Please refer to the section on socialization (page 152) for more on this topic.

II. How to Provide Supports for Impairments of Social Imagination

Impairments of social imagination that emerge as inflexibility, intense special interests, or unusual preferences can cause a variety of problems in everyday life. At the same time, however, they can serve as the perfect opening through which you can confidently provide your child with effective parenting and interventions. Remember that children with impairments of social imagination enjoy certain advantages: they are easily reassured by familiar routines, can readily tap their true potential if they have an accurate expectation of how an activity will unfold, have a great aptitude for memorizing patterns, and are easy to motivate if you appeal to their special interests. I don't think I'm overstating the case by saying that using the impairment of social imagination to advantage is a sine qua non for effectively raising children with autism spectrum disorders.

People often say that we must help these children develop the power to live and the ability to think for themselves. This is true. The problem is that this injunction often comes bundled with the criticism that teaching rote patterns is ineffective, and here I disagree. There are many different ways of developing survival and problem-solving skills. One way—the way that best suits children on the autism spectrum—begins with thinking of memory as a chest of drawers. We fill these drawers with skills and knowledge and then foster the child's ability to judge which to open in a given situation. Less suitable for these individuals is education directed at thinking from scratch without a model or framework. What I am advocating, in short, is utilizing the impairment of social imagination to compensate for the impairment of social imagination.

The Ability to Switch Emotional Gears

Imagine that you are in the toy section of a department store and you say to your child, "Today is your birthday so I will buy you a toy that you like. Go ahead and choose one." But then imagine that your child picks one that is too expensive for you to buy, too big to fit in the house, too difficult for him or her to use, or rather uninteresting and similar to another purchased just recently. So you say, "No, you can't have that one. Pick any one but that one." But your child insists that that is the only toy he or she wants, begins to cry, and then gets angry. You lose your patience and shout, "How can you be so selfish when I have offered to buy you a present? I'm never going to bring you to the department store again!" What you intended to be a happy occasion has been ruined.

Children on the autism spectrum find it extremely difficult to switch after they have made up their minds. Your child was told to choose, but his choice was rejected. You have set him a very cruel task.

To give something up, to be patient, to wait your turn, these are all important issues. But the problem is that even to you, a parent interested in learning about the autism spectrum, difficulty with these skills appears to be a failing of character or willpower. It is also the shortcoming for which you are likely to receive the most criticism from your mother and mother-in-law, who insist that you must, at a minimum, pound these fundamentals of behavior into their grandchild while he or she is still little.

Why is it that neurotypical children are able to exercise patience or wait their turn from a young age? It is because they can predict that even if they cannot have something now, they will be able to have it next time. In fact, they anticipate that if they allow someone else to go first now it will be much easier for them to have a turn next time. They know that the act of giving something up or letting someone else go first has social value, and they understand that by doing this they can obtain the reward of praise. Or they may perceive themselves with pride as behaving like a "big boy" or a "big girl." And once they have made the decision to wait, their minds are fresh and ready for the enjoyment of some other form of entertainment. Difficulties in developmental areas like these—being able to give something up, to be patient, and to wait your turn—are among the issues closely linked to the triad of impairments in socialization, communication, and social imagination.

In the first place, it is better to avoid asking what a child wants and then prohibiting it. The situation described above could be effectively handled in a variety of ways. You could, for example, bring home an advertising flier of toys you approve of, have your child choose one while you are at home together, and then go to make the actual purchase by yourself. Or, if the child is schoolage and old enough to understand sums of money, you could tell him the maximum price you can afford and ask him to choose within that range. Depending on the child's level of development, even just walking past the toy section can be equivalent to saying, "You can have whatever you want," so be careful.

At the same time, however, it is not always possible to delimit the possible choices beforehand. How should you respond when your child has set his or her mind on something and reacts badly to being told it is unattainable? Again, the approach must be suited to the child's developmental stage, because the child's inability to wait or take no for an answer is not caused by a warped nature but rather by the triad of impairments or other autistic characteristics.

It is crucial to make it very clear what the child will gain as a substitute for what he or she gives up. Treating your little one to a drink of juice in order to get away from the toy section, or producing a distraction, such as a favorite candy or toy that you have kept hidden in your bag, are highly appropriate responses for children with autistic characteristics. Although some people may protest that "bribing" a child in this way is sneaky and not true discipline, providing a concrete alternative is an appropriate intervention for children with ASDs who find it difficult to switch gears. When the child's development has progressed to the point where he or she understands when, or under what conditions, a desired item will be attainable, it becomes possible to introduce the goal of being patient until he or she gets it. It is important to take appropriate small steps in order to reach developmental goals.

Until a certain amount of socialization has taken place, it is difficult to teach the social value of being patient when one wants something right now. Of course, there are some children who, even from early childhood, find praise a reward, and in these cases praise is enough compensation for being patient. But, as I pointed out earlier, even children on the high-functioning end of the autism spectrum are often unable to express their true feelings. A common pattern is for such youngsters to put up with a situation simply because they cannot refuse, belying the fact that they do not yet have even the slightest ability to experience pleasure in being patient; this compliance is followed by an explosion upon reaching home, or else stress accumulates to the breaking point, and suddenly everything is rejected. We may end up paying the penalty when the child reaches adolescence or adulthood. It is better to recognize the reality of the impairment of social imagination and to understand that making children with this characteristic be patient for a vague, unlimited period of time is simply not appropriate.

Deriving Power from Transparency

Due to impairment of social imagination, children on the autism spectrum experience strong anxiety in situations where they cannot foresee what will happen next or the final outcome. Some may not be able to distinguish clearly between times when such transparency is possible and times when it is not; this particular difficulty is especially likely to arise when intellectual development is still insufficient or when the child has strong ADHD symptoms, such as impulsivity or high distractibility (see page 93). When a child encounters a situation or activity with low transparency, it is best to assume that this is provoking strong anxiety, even if he or she is smiling or laughing. Anxiety in the face of the unknown may sound like a weakness, but in fact it is merely the flip side of one of their strengths. These same children can easily tap their potential when they can predict what's coming, and if they are satisfied with this game plan they will work twice as hard as anyone else without begrudging the effort. It is easy to reap the advantages of this trait by using visual cues, such as cards or objects, to clearly show children what to expect and to make repeated confirmation possible. The abstract concept of time, which is difficult for children on the autism spectrum to comprehend, can also be made visually clear by checking off each completed item on a schedule chart or putting the

card for that item in a "finished" box. This also allows children to check how far they have progressed overall and how much remains to be done before they reach the goal. Using a schedule in this way to enhance transparency is, in one sense, purposely creating a new perseveration or rigid routine. This method utilizes the impairment of social imagination to compensate for its own negative aspects.

I have heard some people express the concern that creating dependence on a schedule in this way may cause children trouble when they grow up. In fact, however, attachment to a schedule will actually help give them flexibility in daily life. Some parents think, "Our child already has our daily routine down pat, so there's no need for a (written or pictorial) schedule," but this mistaken belief wastes a golden opportunity. Is it practical to try altering a schedule that is firmly fixed in a child's mind? If the schedule is on paper, changes can be visually and repeatedly confirmed. Supported by the routine of following rules such as, "When you finish, put the card in the box" and "When all the cards are finished, it's time for supper," the child is able to accept changes (Schopler, Mesibov and Hearsey 1995). As discussed further on page 144, we can teach flexibility directly by deliberately incorporating "wild card" items into the schedule. Also, a clearly marked chart with the day's schedule allows other people to see what the child is expecting. Depending on the child's developmental level and on family circumstances, it can be helpful for parents to mark their own schedules and display these alongside the child's chart as well in order to prevent misunderstandings and to help yourself remember any promises you have made. Using a visual support for daily planning can reduce discrepancies in expectations.

It is quite common for adults in the professional world to use a Palm Pilot or other electronic planning tool as they organize and go about their day. If advantages can be gained from a tool of this kind that can grow with the child as his or her level of flexibility changes, then why not start young? Some children will stop glancing at their schedule chart once they are accustomed to it and have attained the feeling of security it was intended to provide; at this point they will appear not to be relying on it very much. But it is not wise to rush to remove it. Once it is gone, you may notice that the child becomes visibly anxious. It plays a significant role in reassuring the child that he or she can always look at it to confirm and in reminding the child that he or she has some activity planned. For children on the high-functioning end of the spectrum who have become capable of using written information, the schedule chart can be reduced in size; at this stage, rather than eliminating it altogether it would be best to change its form. Children can also use the schedule chart to practice planning their own schedules in the future.

Respect the Characteristic of Preferring Sameness

Children on the autism spectrum tend to have a wide variety of "rules" in the form of habits governing their behavior, and they vary in their ability to be flexible in applying them. Children who have impairment of social imagination find it immensely reassuring to be able to confirm that things are "just as usual." This is part of their nature, and we should not be trying to eliminate it. "Always brush my teeth before bed," for example, is one rule we should encourage. And later in life: "Always give my wife a gift on our anniversary." What a wonderful rule!

In other words, rules in themselves are not bad. There are only two types of situation in which they can cause difficulties: when they interfere with daily life and when the child is unable to bend them to fit the circumstances.

Concerning the first type, I suggest that you use finesse to guide your child in the direction of an appropriate rule before he or she has established one likely to become a major inconvenience. Again, use the impairment of social imagination to advantage. Many children on the autism spectrum easily develop habits that are beneficial to daily life, such as washing their hands, brushing their teeth, and hanging up their bags and jackets when they arrive at kindergarten. If you present a beneficial habit in a way that is consistent, visual, and easy to understand, you increase the possibility that the child will incorporate the habit into his or her rules. Actively promoting your child's acquisition of such rules not only teaches useful life skills, but also provides reassurance by surrounding him or her with familiar routines in daily life.

If your child does adopt a rule that is very inconvenient, the trick is not to try to eliminate it, but rather to work on replacing it with something more appropriate. For example, you may want to replace, "I must hang my bag at kindergarten on the second hook from the right" with "I must hang my bag at kindergarten on the hook with the airplane mark." The second rule can follow your child from one year to the next, making the annual transition that much easier, and encouraging its adoption is one way to show supportive recognition of your child's craving for routine.

How should we deal with the second point, the inability to apply rules flexibly to fit the circumstances? From the age of three or four, as the child's ability to absorb information from his or her surroundings increases and he becomes more secure in daily life, his insistence on always following established rules often decreases naturally. Just sitting back and waiting for this to happen, however, can lead to problems once he begins spending time in groups at kindergarten, and therefore it is important to provide appropriate interventions to foster flexibility. By intervention I do not mean that you should continuously interfere with what your child wants to do. This will only lead to anxiety and make him or her cling even more insistently to self-styled rules and habits. What I do mean is that you can help your child to match his or her behavior more easily to the needs or requests expressed by others by providing numerous opportunities for developmentally appropriate language reception. Offering regular chances to practice reception successfully is an effective intervention for impairments of both communication and social imagination.

Depending on how much difficulty your child has with social imagination, you can also create practice situations in which you deliberately leave something undecided. Once the use of a schedule has been firmly established, you can introduce a card with a question mark and not reveal its content until you reach that point in the schedule. Be sure to use this "wild card" activity only after careful consideration of your child's present stage of development and current degree of emotional confidence and energy. It is quite common for children on the autism spectrum to be confronted with social imagination activities for which they are not yet fully prepared. People tend to adopt a "one-size-fits-all" mindset when choosing educational goals concerning impairment of social imagination. For instance, they may set targets such as attaining a specific degree of flexibility before entering the school years, or learning to tolerate social ambiguity by the time they reach adulthood. Interventions need to be individualized and based on each child's current developmental needs.

Responding to Restricted Interests

I have already explained that children on the autism spectrum show strongly biased interests in specific objects or activities. People often ask me how these can be eliminated. While some consult me because their child's limited repertoire is interfering with daily life and preventing him or her from developing broader interests, others tell me frankly that they find this behavior too painful to watch because it is so obviously autistic.

The fact that the child has objects or activities in which he is strongly interested is, however, a very important vehicle that can be used to further his or her education. If the trains a child loves are incorporated in a lesson plan, he (or she) may quite eagerly learn letters or mathematical concepts or become engrossed in work that requires fine motor skills, which are usually quite difficult for children with ASDs to master. Rather than trying to eliminate restricted interests, I suggest making rules to prevent them from interfering with the daily life of your child and the rest of the family or other people with whom he or she interacts. For example, if your child collects boxes of detergent and runs out of places to keep them, you could put a new twist on this special interest by making a special set of shelves for his detergent collection. You could then fill the shelves with twenty storage bins and establish the following agreement with your child: "You may choose twenty boxes of detergent and put each one into its own basket and display them on the shelves. You may not keep any more than twenty, but you may take photos of additional boxes and keep them in a photo album." The important point when doing this is to take into consideration the characteristics of autism and present the new rule in a way that is easy to accept and also easy to understand visually. Depending on the level of development, some children may be able to handle less specific rules such as "We will buy the next one when we have used up this one." Or, to save space, you may be able to sell them on the idea of "collecting" knowledge—for instance, handwritten copies of the ingredients labels from detergent boxes—rather than the actual objects.

It is important to remember that children on the autism spectrum have just as much right as anyone to enjoy doing the things they like. People have highly diverse interests and ways of expressing them. Take, for example, the Japanese graphic designer and artist Tadanori Yokoo, who loves painting forked roads, or the Japanese stage designer Kappa Senoo, who enjoys researching and writing about toilets in famous people's houses. And then there is the Japanese hobby of collecting the paper wrappers used on bullet train boxed lunches. All of these are wonderful. Even someone who has no interest in forked roads, for example, may be inspired to take a look when he sees someone so enthusiastic about them. You have been given the chance to become the first person to understand your "little scholar." Most children will replace one special interest with another after a few years of intense involvement. We should leave children to decide what that interest will be, and in any case trying to force a change will only increase the intensity of absorption. If, however, a child has taken up something obviously inappropriate, such as collecting knives or cutting up small animals, then we must try to get him or her to find something new. Does the

child like knives because they are shiny? Or because he likes tools, or historical things? Is there something else that might capture his or her fancy instead? Interests that are out of control are sometimes a child's response to the feeling that he or she has no place to turn (see the next section). I have found that children who lack a sense of security and achievement in daily life tend to be more attracted by strong stimuli such as knives and violence. In some cases, the solution lies in reassessing the child's daily life in a general way rather than dealing directly with the behavior itself.

When Rules and Restricted Interests Intensify

In order to establish a personal rule, you have to have enough intelligence to remember it. It is very unusual to see distinct rules or especially strong interests in children before the age of eighteen months. Even this is very early, with inclinations toward this kind of behavior usually becoming more obvious between the ages of two and three. This may be the most difficult period of all for parents. In most cases, problems with handling children at this stage tend to worsen no matter what parents do. But seen from a more positive perspective, when the penchant for specific interests and rules become more pronounced it means that the child has become more teachable; at this point, you can begin to teach him or her appropriate rules, using the underlying triad of impairments to advantage. Once you reach this stage, your trial is almost over. Soon you will see the light at the end of the tunnel.

There are times when a child, after growing older, reverts to a rule that he had previously given up, or intense engagement with a particular object is revived. Such a resurgence can be a sign that the child is facing intense anxiety, so that he or she feels a need to cling to these behaviors. Restricted interests and rules are symptoms of the autism spectrum. But their intensity is not fixed and can easily be heightened or reduced depending on the child's environment or the appropriateness of the tasks demanded of him or her. We must therefore be flexible in how we respond during these periods. During especially stressful times, such as the beginning of a new school year or the second trimester, when there are often many extra school events and activities, we should constructively build habits into the child's daily routine as reassurance, as a means of helping him or her recover and regain steady footing. This could include, for example, allowing more time for immersion in special interests, or reviving the habit of checking the schedule for the following day if this habit has fallen by the wayside. There are also times when autistic symptoms such as rigid behavior, monologues, and so on grow more pronounced without any apparent external trigger. The child might, for example, have recently passed through the initial confusion of entering kindergarten and be acquiring new skills every day. His teacher breathes a sigh of relief and expresses confidence that things are going well, yet at home the child seems to be regressing. At times like this, I suggest reassessing his or her life in general. For example, look at kindergarten. Is your child being given clues that are appropriate for his or her level of language comprehension? Is he or she able to express such thoughts as, "I don't like that" or "I need help"? Has the kindergarten provided space and time for simply relaxing? If your child is put at ease and finds life at kindergarten agreeable, the symptoms will improve. If, however, the child is forced to endure a lifestyle where expectations continually surpass his or her ability for a long period of time, damage in the form of secondary emotional disorders may result, and it may take much more time to heal these wounds than it took to inflict them.

Should we Teach Make-believe Play?

Because of the impairment of social imagination, children on the autism spectrum tend to exhibit insufficiencies in the development of pretend play. Although there are many autistic children who love playing house or who become totally absorbed in superheroes such as Spider-man, their make-believe games are fixed patterns that do not involve reciprocity or the sharing of imagination or plot development with others (see also page 64).

Is it possible to teach such children how to play make-believe games if we start in early childhood? Personally, I do not think they will ever adopt what we think of as "proper" make-believe play. The forms of pretend play they can develop are those that fit the cognitive characteristics of the autism spectrum. When I watch a child spending over thirty minutes developing an elaborate story all by himself as he moves a variety of soldier dolls, I cannot help but think that this, too, is one genuine form of play. Sometimes I become so absorbed in the game that I find myself wondering whether he will grow up to be a movie director or a writer. I do not think that we can judge which is better or "right": our form of make-believe play or that of children on the autism spectrum.

But still, for children on the high-functioning end of the spectrum who must interact with neurotypical children whether they like it or not, it will be more convenient to know how to play the type of make-believe games played by the majority. Teaching make-believe play patterns is very similar to teaching action songs (page 117). It confers some of the same advantages and, in addition, helps the children who are taught feel more familiar with the actions of their preschool peers. In some cases, a child with an ASD might even look on and think, "I want to do that, too, so I might as well join in."

Make-believe play patterns that are repetitive and have a fixed order are surprisingly easy and fun for high-functioning children on the autism spectrum, for example pretending to pour some juice while saying, "Here, have some juice," "Glug, glug, glug," "Ah, it's delicious," and then smiling at each other. Or pretending to take a cookie from a picture in a book and munch on it or say, "Here. You try some." If the child is playing with an adult he trusts, such as his parent, this can be a good opportunity to practice flexibility where the child learns to enjoy the game even when the parent puts a number of different patterns into play during the same session. Different ways of expanding the story might include the addition of "May I have some more?" "I'd like some milk instead, please," and "I'm full. Time to take a bath." If the child likes participating in such games, make-believe play can be included as a style of learning that parent and child can enjoy together.

Tell them when it's Over

The patterns of make-believe play above are, in a sense, perseverative behavior patterns that require the company of other people. Sometimes I meet parents who spend so much time playing pretend games with their child that I feel sorry for them. This happens because the child becomes too absorbed to stop. When we teach children something that is fun to do, we should also try to teach them how to bring that activity to an end. Impairment of social imagination makes it hard for children with ASDs to acquire an abstract sense of the passage of time. Even children who can read a clock or who dwell on the subject of time find it hard to share with others the feeling that "we've been doing this for a very long time." Impairment of social imagination also makes it difficult for children on the autism spectrum to switch from one activity to another. This means that it is quite hard for them to stop an activity they enjoy. An opportunity to teach children how to play something enjoyable is also an excellent opportunity to teach them how to finish "as planned." Children need to practice how to finish an activity that they enjoy in a way that matches their level of development. Some examples include planning an activity that is easy for them to switch to, such as snack time or a favorite TV program, singing the same song at the end of the activity, or using a special timer with visual cues, such as dwindling lights or colours, to indicate clearly how much time is left.[1]

If a child insists that other family members participate in make-believe play to the point where it disrupts daily life, it is important to stop and assess whether this might be caused by anxiety about daily life, by a need to experience a sense of accomplishment, or by lack of sufficient time to play alone.

---

1   Time Timers (produced by the American company Time Timer) are the most representative of these timers. The company also produces a wristwatch version. These and similar products from other companies can be purchased online (see www.timelines.com).

III. Skills that Compensate for Impaired Socialization

Like problems with expressive communication, people tend to think that problems with socialization can be solved by an increase in the quantity of interaction. When a child who has previously shown no interest in others begins to hug or kiss his teacher or other children, this is often mistakenly seen as a step forward, and even a child's efforts to force others to play his or her games may seem heartwarming. But if these inappropriate interactions increase, life will become even more difficult for this child than it is for a child who also has an ASD but is less sociable. Difficulties may be apparent right from early childhood and throughout the school years, or the seriousness of the problem may only be realized when the child reaches adulthood.

With impaired socialization, we must be determined not to use the quantity of interaction with others to gauge developmental progress. We must not lose sight of our objective: to increase appropriate interaction and discourage inappropriate interaction. Handling impairment of socialization by simply throwing a child in with other youngsters entails a high risk. It is extremely difficult to correct inappropriate behavior that a child desperately acquires in order to survive within a group—behaviors such as making noise in order to get attention, making strange sounds or using physical force to refuse or demand something, or hugging and kissing others regardless of their feelings or convenience.

Can Socialization be Taught?

If the term "socialization" simply means not behaving socially inappropriately, then perhaps it can be taught. Some children on the high-functioning end of the autism spectrum can identify inappropriate behavior using their own knowledge of what is appropriate, correct it, and independently expand their repertoire of appropriate behaviors.

In reality, however, socialization is not merely a "how-to" list. It is, instead, the ability to adopt appropriate behavior naturally even when encountering a situation for the first time, informed by the "common sense" of your peer group or the "unspoken agreement" of that social situation. It also means being able to sense the feelings of another person from the mood that the individual exudes or from social common sense, and to empathize with these feelings. And it means having your way of experiencing emotions empathized with by others without a sense of incongruity. If socialization is equivalent to having these abilities, it is probably impossible for children on the autism spectrum to fundamentally improve their weakness in this area.

What we can teach these children is patterns of information concerning how most people in our society feel and act and the skill to select behaviors that match. This is very different from the socialization process of neurotypical children.

It is extremely difficult to train very young children on the autism spectrum in skills that compensate for impaired socialization because the impairment has not yet caused them significant distress or inconvenience. Although they are already being kept at arm's length by others and are losing out on the enjoyment of social interaction, their social impairment makes it hard for them to realize that the cause is their own lack of knowhow.

Development of Social Interaction is Not a Matter of Quantity

Impaired social interaction is difficult to express in quantitative terms and therefore hard to grasp. People tend to think that it can be improved with the accumulation of experience, through exhortations, or by demanding that the child behave in an age-appropriate way, but they are mistaken. Many people also equate the development of social interaction with an overall increase in interactions with other people. Once again, this assumption is incorrect. If a twenty-year-old male suddenly embraced a woman passing him on the street or picked up a child he did not know, his behavior would certainly be considered maladjusted.

The development of social interaction means both an increase in appropriate interaction with others and no increase in inappropriate interaction. People on the autism spectrum who do not know what is socially acceptable tend to develop their own ways of interacting and behaving. Inappropriate interaction not only makes life difficult for everyone involved, but it can also inspire fear in others or be seen as criminal behavior, as in the case of physical contact such as embracing members of the opposite sex or picking up children one does not know.

Because it is difficult to identify inappropriate behavior during early childhood, people tend to focus solely on increasing the amount of interaction. But we should always keep in mind the child's future as an adult. Even adults who spend comparatively little time interacting with others, choosing instead to spend private time immersed in something that interests them, are perfectly capable of participating in society as long as they can interact appropriately at work and do not engage in inappropriate behavior. In contrast, those who do interact appropriately in professional situations but make unwelcome attempts to spend time with coworkers during breaks or outside of office hours will find it difficult to fit in at work.

By preventing children on the autism spectrum from developing inappropriate behavior patterns as they grow, we are aiding the development of social interaction. It is extremely important for us as supporters of these children to recognize that this type of support is not the same as making great increases in degree of interaction.

Approaching another person, talking to others, or making eye contact—all of these actions can be quantified and therefore they are often used in medical and psychological studies as indicators of development in social interaction. However, I caution you against unquestioning acceptance of the results of programs that are based on increasing the volume of interaction. Rather, you should first assess whether there is any risk that these programs will increase the amount of inappropriate interaction. Claims that even children with obviously impaired intellectual development or conspicuous symptoms of autism should be admitted to mainstream school classrooms, where the increased stimulation will foster social interaction, are typical of misguided approaches that fail to address the essential goal of preventing increases in inappropriate interaction. I have seen too many children who have been crushed and ostracized because this approach to intervention has subjected them to endless days of anxiety and confusion by aggravating rigid interests or routines and hypersensitivity and increasing inappropriate interaction.

When a child who formerly showed no interest in others begins to seek contact, parents tend to welcome this behavior, no matter how one-sided and inappropriate it may be. I do not wish to belittle the joy that parents feel at this change. It is indeed a sign of development. Such behavior demonstrates that the child who formerly did not even notice the existence of other human beings has now become aware of an entity known as "people."

However, not all the behaviors that result from this newfound awareness are ones that we want the child to keep. To head out the front door all alone and make a beeline for the train station, to slip through the ticket gate and get on a fascinating train… Such actions would be impossible without cognitive development. But it is not behavior that we want the child to repeat. There are some behaviors that we must eliminate or discourage before they occur, even if they do accompany growth. Rigid patterns that involve others will not evolve into reciprocity. It is therefore important to treat such behaviors as inappropriate and detrimental to developing social interaction. We can begin supporting appropriate interaction by first revising the approach that assesses development by the quantity of interaction with others.

The Importance of Objects as Clues

If they are provided with prompts appropriate to their autistic characteristics and to their level of intellectual development, children on the high-functioning end of the spectrum can learn to use such prompts spontaneously. For example, they can learn to check and follow a schedule board to determine what they're supposed to be doing. This kind of independence—as opposed to reliance on other people as clues to appropriate social behavior—is extremely important and will not interfere with the development of social or communication skills. Rather, the experience gained through self-directed behavioral choices will support development. Certainly, for some children a desirable goal is to acquire the ability to evaluate their behavior by reading people's faces. But such fuzzy, amorphous clues as facial expressions are difficult to understand and can make children with ASDs anxious. The notion that they can figure out what to do by imitating others or by being told may result in a child who always waits for instructions or one who has no self-confidence.

Children who have learned to move in perfect sync with one teacher may be thrown into confusion following a change in personnel. This tragedy is frequently experienced when a child begins a new school year with a new teacher after having had a teacher who simply had an intuitive knack for discerning and meeting that child's needs. Children who can use objects as clues, however, can use this skill across different settings—for instance, when their teacher changes. A really good instructor is one whose perennial presence is unnecessary, because he or she has taught the child skills that can be used independently. In short, the ability to use objects as clues will help the child develop lasting social skills that are his very own.

Begin with Rules and Instructions for Appropriate Behavior

Most preschoolers with ASDs, even if they are high functioning, are not yet at the level where they can identify on their own what behavior is appropriate in a specific situation. An important target is to be able to accept the necessity of certain social behaviors that have been clearly modelled and to use these behaviors by themselves and without becoming confused.

Specific teaching goals include enabling the child to accurately understand information about appropriate behavior, ask for help by an appropriate means (e.g., saying, "Please show me" instead of screaming or running away), and communicate any objections or problems by appropriate means (e.g., saying, "I want to skip my turn," or "Let me go last"). In other words, socialization targets are to some extent inseparable from communication targets.

If it is taking a long time for a child to acquire these kinds of behaviors, then we should examine whether we have taken appropriate measures to deal with impairments of communication (for example, are we giving information in a form that is easy for the child to comprehend) and social imagination (for example, are we giving sufficient consideration to difficulty with switching gears), and whether we are utilizing the child's high capacity for repetitive pattern memorization. Common parental mistakes are excessive verbal communication, insufficient information in the form of prompts, and lack of consistency.

Filling Memory Files with Appropriate Behaviors Versus Trial and Error

During the preschool years, we should be aiming to fill children's "memory files" with appropriate social behaviors. Children on the high-functioning end of the autism spectrum often do not need constant instruction on how to behave appropriately; instead, they can discern the social signals themselves and access the appropriate memory file spontaneously. For example, they may see the signal "The teacher is standing at the front of the room" and retrieve the

file that says, "The teacher may be about to say something, so I should look at her." In a place where "everyone is silent," they may retrieve the file that says, "I'd better be quiet, too," even if they cannot actually share the feeling of quietude. In other words, children can learn to select appropriate social behavior independently, even without an improvement in the impairment in socialization per se. But like the boy Michitaka introduced in Chapter 1, sometimes a child may open the wrong file. For example, in response to the situation "The teacher has asked me the same question again" he may choose a file that says, "Try randomly choosing a different answer." Or in response to the situation "The teacher didn't tell me, 'Yes; good answer!'" he may open a file with the instructions, "Just keep on talking; anything will do." In these cases, what we really want is for the child to find files that instruct him to stop and think, "Did I say something wrong?" or "I don't really know what to say."

Due to the impairment of social imagination, children on the autism spectrum find it difficult to correct mistaken impressions, and children who are left to their own devices to discover things by trial and error frequently find themselves trapped in their own assumptions, causing suffering to themselves and those around them. Not only is it more effective to give them clear instructions or to model appropriate behavior at the beginning, it will also reduce the amount of stress on your child. To summarize, taking advantage of the ability to work from stored memories is an approach tailored to many children on the autism spectrum.

Don't be Too Quick to Increase Time Spent in Peer Groups

Believing that impaired socialization can be improved by thrusting their child into groups of other children, some mothers go to the park every day when they know it will be most crowded, steeling themselves for the ordeal as if it were ascetic training. But when they get there, their child plays alone in the sand or with water or runs around solo; interactions with other children consist only of grabbing or knocking down their toys. To show how sorry they are, the mothers may yell at their child or even swat them. I do not believe that it is necessary to force a child at this stage of development to go where there are many other children. Instead, see those trips to the park as a way to refresh yourselves, to help your child recognize a clearly defined daily routine, to burn up energy, or to give your child experience exercising. It is important to accept these steps as positive achievements. For children at this stage, the best teachers are not their peers, but rather adults who are able to toss experiential "balls" that are easy enough for them to catch (see page 109). There is no need to be concerned if your child does not spend much time with his or her peers. As mentioned earlier, spending long periods of time in groups that lack a clear structure in terms of rules or procedures will not necessarily improve socialization.

Peer Groups as a Whirlwind of Distress

Have you ever been in a group of twenty or thirty children all playing freely? With children screaming and creating commotion on all sides, the noise is incredible. Neurotypical children in kindergarten and early elementary school are also only beginning to develop social skills, and consequently their actions tend to be very self-centred in an entirely age-appropriate way. In a group, they generate a flood of sound and motion, and it is impossible to predict what will happen from one moment to the next. It is not unusual for children on the autism spectrum to experience this atmosphere as a whirlwind of unpredictable and distressing stimuli. Considering that they also have impairments of social imagination and communication as well as sensory issues, this is only natural. The fact that they are totally exhausted by such excessive stimuli is a completely separate issue from whether they actually want to play with other children or not.

Group social experience is important, and we should take care to prevent these opportunities from becoming unpleasant and encroaching upon the child's life to the point where he or she feels under siege. Too many negative experiences can lead children on the autism spectrum to refuse social contact altogether. We need to provide supports that are appropriate for each child's individual stage of development, including adult intervention and mechanisms for increasing transparency of expectations. At times when we are not able to provide supports during recess or other blocks of free time, we should ensure that children with ASDs have a place to be on their own and an appropriate play activity. If there's one thing we should engrave in our minds, it's this: targets such as "making friends as soon as possible" or "making lots of friends" are inappropriate, no matter what the age of the child.

When Should Mainstream Education Begin?

Up to this point, I have stressed the danger of placing children in peer groups without providing any supports. But by no means do I intend to imply that mainstream education is inappropriate no matter what the situation. My intention instead is to sound a warning against the belief, which is deeply ingrained in our society, that mainstream education is unequivocally good for every child and that every child should attend a kindergarten or day care centre.[2] These assertions, which do not consider the individual, are meaningless overgeneralizations.

If both parents are working, preschool education is obviously appropriate. It is generally easier for day care centres and kindergartens to provide children with a stable routine than it is for the children's grandparents, who might alternatively be asked to care for them during the day. Childcare workers and early childhood educators have unparalleled expertise at teaching such self-care skills as independently dressing and using the toilet, and if you can get the teachers to understand the nature of autism, there are many advantages to sending your child to such a facility. It would be ideal if the teachers followed the kind of advice I've been suggesting throughout this book: carefully identifying the level of instruction that your child can comprehend, providing a clear framework, and not forcing him or her to interact with others. Those responsible for the care of high-functioning children on the autism spectrum will need to engage in extra study outside of working hours and will also need extra hands and eyes in the classroom. Responsibility for decisions concerning the care and education of such children will be a heavy burden, both logistically and emotionally, for the classroom teacher or childcare worker to bear alone. There are some

---

2   The typical Japanese day care center (*hoikuen*) accepts children from birth to six years of age. While utilized primarily by families with working mothers, they are also often lauded for their assistance with the goals of early socialization and the early acquisition of skills; it is possible, therefore, that *hoikuen* have a more positive image than do day care centers in Western countries.

cases in which public day care centres or kindergartens can get support from the local government (see page 204). Some teachers may hesitate to bring up the subject of applying for this type of assistance, and therefore it is a good idea for parents to take the initiative and let the school or centre know that they would like to pursue this avenue if their district has such provisions.

Almost every child on the high-functioning end of the spectrum will be attending a kindergarten or day care centre once they've reached the age of four. At the beginning of Chapter 2 (page 106) I explained that interventions in early childhood should be a part of everyday life at home. Daily intervention in a kindergarten or other preschool setting does not mean individualized academic instruction. Rather it means providing supports that are suited to autistic characteristics and are designed to help children handle daily life smoothly, with confidence and self-esteem. One meaningful intervention is the very act of sending the child to preschool, to the extent that it is a place outside the home where the child can relax and have pleasant experiences with adults capable of creating such an environment.

Some experts advise parents to begin kindergarten or day care as early as possible in order to accelerate socialization, but I personally do not agree with this view, for reasons I have already explained. It is not how early a child begins kindergarten or day care, but rather the quality of the time spent there that is important. Of course, the situation in the home may necessitate an early start. Not all mothers can interact well with their children if they are with them all day long. They may do much better if their time together is divided over the course of the day. This has nothing to do with whether a mother loves her child or not. If spending the entire day together causes a parent to feel pressured, or if it is detrimental to the parent's relationship with the child's siblings, then kindergarten and day care settings can be very useful in establishing a stable daily routine.

Can Appropriate Peer Interaction be Taught?

Sometimes parents consult me about problems concerning peer interaction. "I'm really worried about my child because he throws his arms around his friends when he wants them to play with him. If I could at least teach him to say, 'Can I play, too?'" But this is a very difficult issue. Although people tend to see it as a matter of learning how to ask for something (an issue of expressive communication), in almost every case it is in fact a problem of socialization rather than of expression.

What if that child did learn how to say, "Can I play, too?" The fact that he runs up and grabs his friends when he wants to play indicates that he does not realize that others have their own agendas and that he himself has times when, even if he wants to play, he cannot. It will surely be hard for him to forgive a classmate who won't play with him after he's made the effort to follow the rule and ask in words. As a result, the child will find himself even more of an outsider. Children with ASDs who are better at speaking than at listening are not necessarily well accepted by their typically developing peers. It must be remembered that these classmates are also trying to work their way through childhood and have their own needs, so this is more than just a one-dimensional problem of atypical children being singled out and excluded because of their differences.

Depending upon the level of development, it is possible to create situations in which children on the high-functioning end of the autism spectrum can play with their peers without being excluded. Conditions that make participation easier are games or other playtime activities with clear rules. These include taking turns on the slide and playing tag or musical chairs. Preschool children with higher than average intelligence can also play cards or board games and learn to follow the rules (such as "Don't get angry or cheat even if you are losing"). These games have the advantage of making it easy for adults to intervene. Unexpected trouble is an inherent feature of interaction between children in general, but when a child with an ASD is involved, the situation will be less likely to get out of hand if an adult intervenes at an early stage, rather than leaving the children to work things out on their own.

Impairments in socialization are a more central issue from adolescence onward than they are in early childhood. It is best to approach these difficulties as a long-term theme lasting right up until adulthood and to deal with them one step at a time. The important thing is not the amount of experience, but rather the accumulation of pleasant experiences and the limiting of unpleasant experiences associated with group participation.

One Approach that can Help Children Accept Social Rules

With children who have higher than average intelligence, it may also be possible to deal with their way of thinking a little more directly. This approach entails explaining to a child why he or she should or should not do something in a way that respects the framework of autistic thinking and that the child can therefore understand and accept. Let me give you two examples.

Example 1: Six-year-old Takashi is very precise and obeys rules faithfully. One day on the way home from his day care centre, he suddenly runs up to the crosswalk and shouts, "Red means stop!" A businessman who had ignored the stoplight and was making a dash for the train station turns to stare at Takashi, as do many other people on their way to do some shopping.

Mother: "You're right, Takashi. Red means stop. You remembered that rule very well."

Takashi: "A policewoman came to class and taught us."

Mother: "That's right. But you know, Takashi, everyone was very surprised right now, and they were staring at you."

Takashi: "Because that man crossed on a red light."

Takashi's mother takes out a pencil and paper and begins to write.

Mother: "Takashi, look at this. Number 1, red means stop. That's a rule, just like you said. But did you know that there is another rule? Number 2, don't talk to adults you don't know. Of these two, rule number 2 is more important than rule number 1. Number 1 gets one star. Number 2 gets two stars. So from now on, it would be better if you didn't warn men you don't know, even if they cross on a red light. Hey, Takashi, now you've learned another rule. Good for you!"

"Rule number 2, don't talk to adults you don't know," Takashi repeats to himself, in surprise. "All right, I've got it now. I've got a new rule to add to my collection."

Example 2: Chisa, a fifth grader, is good at logical thinking, but she tends to be a quibbler. One day, her mother finishes some straightening up and then joins her at the table, where she is eating donuts. "Chisa," she asks, "may I have a donut please?" Chisa picks up a doughnut and tosses it. "Nice catch," she says, but her mother looks very stern.

Mother: "Chisa! That's rude."

Chisa: "But I gave you one, just like you asked."

Mother: "You should not throw food. That's just common sense."

Chisa: "But you get your donut faster if I throw it. And I don't even have to get off my chair. It's very convenient."

Realizing that her daughter is being quite sincere, Chisa's mother changes tactics.

Mother: "Yes, you're right. What you are saying is really true. But if I hadn't caught it, it would have fallen on the floor, got dirty, and made a mess."

Chisa is taken aback.

Mother: "Also, many people think it's rude to throw food, because it's as if you're feeding a dog. There is a big chance that people will think you don't know how to be polite if you do that. Even though I know that what you are thinking is correct, please don't do it any more, because I don't want people to misunderstand you."

"I get it!" says Chisa. "Thanks, Mom. I had no idea people would think I was clueless about manners just because of something like that. It's like there was some secret that I just didn't know about." And she resolved not to throw food any more.

Neither Takashi nor Chisa ever repeated these behaviors. But this type of logic does not work with every child on the high-functioning end of the autism spectrum. There may be some for whom this style of teaching is not suitable. And although there is definitely such a thing as "autistic thinking," it differs slightly for each individual. It is precisely because these mothers knew their children very well that they could choose an argument that would click at that particular moment. The important thing is to respect the child's reasoning. Responding with "It's more convenient to throw food?! That's ridiculous!" will get you nowhere. Throwing is definitely convenient. Perhaps it was someone like Chisa who invented the conveyor belt. But more important, the fact that she focuses on the convenience is neither good nor bad: it is just the way she is.

One time, I was doing Show and Tell as part of a group session with elementary school children who have Asperger's Syndrome, and I joined the children in presenting something special and explaining it to the group. I chose a book printed on cheap, coarse paper just after World War II by one of Japan's venerable old publishing houses. "This book was given to me thirty-five years ago by my favorite uncle," I explained. I then asked them if they had any questions, expecting that at least one of them would ask about my uncle. "I do! How big is the font of the letters in that book?" "How many pages does the book have?" "Tell me the names of the characters in the book." I was intrigued: "Oh! So that's the angle they take," I thought to myself. The response of most people would be to ask about the presenter's favorite uncle, whereas these atypical children couldn't imagine starting anywhere else but by first checking the point size, the number of pages, or the names of the main characters. It is not a matter of which is right. We cannot tell them, "The first thing you should be interested in is my uncle." After all, people are free to think and feel as they will. Instead, the kind of message we can send them is this: "Wow, so that's what caught your attention first. I would never have thought of that. You should know, for what it's worth, that in this situation most people would start by asking about my uncle first." But of course, this kind of instruction should only be supplied when it is really necessary.

The social skills of our society conform to "our" logic—the logic of the majority, or the typical population. For children on the autism spectrum, they no doubt seem illogical and hard to get used to. When we attempt to teach them about social skills, we must always keep this point in mind. When we attempt to foster social skills, what we are really doing is asking these youngsters to behave in a way that is compatible with our logic and giving them the techniques to do so. We are saying, in effect, "I respect the legitimacy of your feelings and way of thinking, but your life, and the lives of those around you, will be easier if you have the skills to adapt to the logic of the majority. Please do your best" (Wing and Yoshida 2005).

Cognitive therapy, a psychiatric technique used with adults, aims at changing the way a person interprets experiences—his or her so-called cognitive structure. The approach I described above is fundamentally different from classic cognitive therapy. We are not trying to change children's cognitive structure. We begin with the premise that this will not change and instead help them to learn, in an academic sort of way, about how the majority of people perceive things. Our reason for teaching this is not that their way is wrong, but rather that the knowledge will mean less inconvenience both for them and for us. It is important that both the therapist and the child be aware of this.

As I'm sure you understand, this approach is too difficult for all but a very few exceptional children of preschool or early elementary school age. This kind of teaching is impossible until the child desires to understand the logic of society at large or else becomes aware that he or she does not know as much about it as other people seem to. Sufficient language comprehension is a prerequisite. This approach also carries the risk of deteriorating into a quibbling match with a single misstep.

So why have I included in this book a discussion that is really more relevant for older children, for those who are at least in upper elementary school? Because I wanted to convey what it means to teach children on the autism spectrum "social skills." Having this information in hand is part of your preparation for the future, when the time comes that you and others supporting your child will be able to make use of it.

IV. Helping Daily Life Run Smoothly: Frequently Asked Questions

We must consider a child's developmental characteristics in order to remove difficulties from his or her daily life. If any steps you take produce positive results in this respect, consider yourself to have successfully implemented an intervention for your child. Interventions should be a part of everyday life. We should avoid being too confined by preconceptions about what is considered "age-appropriate" discipline and instead look at the individual child's level of development and specific autistic characteristics. This will tell us what we should be doing in terms of choosing targets and the means by which to work toward those targets. Details of what constitutes the most appropriate way forward will differ from child to child and from family to family. In this section, I answer questions frequently asked by parents; my responses, taken as a whole, are intended as just one example of how to develop your own approach to providing your child with supportive interventions.

When we go to the park, my child spends the whole time just running around and acts "wired." What should I do?

This type of concern is frequently voiced by parents of preschoolers and younger school-aged children. Related to hyperactivity, it includes such complaints as "If I let go of his hand, he takes off and I don't know where he's gone," "He runs out into the street and it's really dangerous," and "He can never seem to settle down." These worries are serious, because behavior like this threatens the safety of the child and sometimes of other children as well.

Below I have listed some possible causes for hyperactive behavior. They are not mutually exclusive, and in most cases more than one is involved. Seen from the perspective of the child, hyperactive behavior is an attempt to fulfil some legitimate need. Simply to demand that he or she be still without removing the cause is as unreasonable as suddenly ordering someone to sit in the lotus position and meditate when that person knows nothing about the purpose or benefits of meditation.

First, identify what is causing your child to act "wired" and then think about how to deal with it. A number of possible causes are described below.

The Distraction of Too Many Stimuli

Children on the autism spectrum tend to be strongly distracted by things that can be seen (visual stimuli) and heard (auditory stimuli). If your child is fairly calm at home, but hyperactive behavior increases noticeably when you go to the department store or an amusement park, or during recess at kindergarten, it may well be that he or she is feeling a sort of inner chaos because of an inability to process excessive stimuli.

In addition, one characteristic of the autism spectrum is the existence of specific interests that are impossible to suppress when the child is tempted by the sight (or sound) of something that acts as a trigger. To command your child to "Calm down!" or to say "Don't touch that!" without removing the distracting and attractive stimuli is like demanding that someone stick to a diet while you cover the table with a smorgasbord of his favorite, fattening foods. We should first remove the cause of temptation from sight.

The first step in intervention is to organize and tidy the home. It is very difficult to maintain a perfectly neat home, with everything in its place, when you are in the middle of raising children. But the attempt is worth every effort. Steel yourself to throw away anything for which you have no storage space. Remove any pictures, ornaments, or advertisements you have stuck to the fridge or walls. Store toys on a designated set of shelves in boxes that are sized to fit neatly on those shelves. (If you maintain this arrangement, it will become a very convenient way to teach your child to put away his or her own things.) The amount of stimuli can be significantly reduced by simply concealing messy shelves behind a single plain curtain. The one time of day when sitting down should be insisted upon is mealtime. Therefore, it is especially important to make sure that there are no temptations visible from where your child is sitting during the meal. One curtain is worth more than one hundred rebukes! When your child is no longer distracted by unnecessary stimuli, it will be easier for him or her to concentrate on the stimulus you want to draw attention to, such as the sound of your voice. Controlling excessive stimuli is also a way to support the development of communication and social skills.

You may believe that taking your child to places with a large amount of stimuli is necessary for developmental progress, but such outings are unnecessary. In fact, it will be impossible for your child to process the excessive sensory stimulation to which he or she is exposed in a way that furthers development. Outings that are enjoyable for your child and refreshing for all of you, including the child's siblings, however, are not a problem.

It is possible, with some children, to work toward the goal of the child's being able to endure some degree of temptation. But we must realize that this is in fact quite an advanced goal and remember to proceed with great caution, carefully weighing whether it is an appropriate step or not.

Confusion about What Behavior is Expected

Children often become unsettled if they do not know what they are supposed to be doing at a given moment. This is frequently the reason children will get up and wander around during class soon after entering kindergarten or elementary school. It is also frequently why hyperactive behavior may resume at the start of any new school year, even though the previous year the child had settled down without intervention after the first two or three months. The behavior had subsided because the child had managed to memorize, in his or her own way, the details of the daily routine. In cases like these, if the methods of instruction are not reassessed, periods of hyperactive behavior are likely to recur with each transition.

Reasons why children may not know what they are supposed to be doing:

★ They have not received clear instructions (e.g., the outline for a certain activity or block of time is unclear; they do not know what to do during recess or other free periods).

★ They could not understand the instructions (refer to page 51 concerning communication).

★ They were not paying attention to the instructions (e.g., they were distracted by something else and did not see or hear the teacher giving instructions. Keep excessive stimuli under control on a daily basis and begin giving instructions only after getting the child's attention).

Anxiety or Lack of Motivation Because the Situation is Not Transparent

Due to impairments of social imagination, it is difficult for children on the autism spectrum to prepare themselves mentally to adjust to a new situation or new instructions. They may understand what you've asked them to do, but cannot motivate themselves to comply, often because they are uncertain about where this will lead in the end. See the section on responding to impairments of social imagination (page 136) for ideas on helping children to get ready for a transition before you actually ask them to make it. Children with ASDs don't like surprises, and their inability to switch gears can cause them to become hyperactive.

Inability to Maintain Concentration and Pay Attention

If the length, degree of difficulty, level of interest, level of distraction, and other factors are not appropriate to the child's level of development, then he or she will be unable to maintain concentration and may act "wired" or flighty. Appropriate interventions are the same as those suggested in response to the following question concerning deliberate misbehavior (page 176).

Physiological Distress

Physiological distress as a cause of hyperactive behavior is most common in children who have accompanying intellectual impairments, but it can also occur in some children—especially younger ones—on the high-functioning end of the spectrum. Children can become unsettled by a cold or other illness, a lack of sleep, constipation or diarrhoea, and so on.

We have just examined the issue of hyperactive behavior. But there are children who, under circumstances like those described above, will either freeze up or cry. To those witnessing the episode, these reactions may seem very different from the case of children becoming "wired," but the proper response is very similar. We need to pay careful attention to children who react in these ways as well. Their need for a response is more easily overlooked because they are less disruptive than those who become hyperactive.

My child behaves badly on purpose while looking straight at me. Should I scold him or just ignore him?

Children on the high-functioning end of the autism spectrum often show interest in other people from an early age, although their approaches are usually one-sided. It is not uncommon for them to misbehave, for example by deliberately stepping out of line and running away laughing, knowing full well that the teacher will reprimand them; grabbing a toy from another's hand in the expectation that the playmate will get mad and yell, "Give it back!"; spitting at someone while laughing; butting people with their heads; deliberately dropping things; and so on. Prevention is key, but when these behaviors do occur, examine the cause and take immediate action. Let's look at three possible reasons for this kind of behavior, beginning with the most common.

Perseverative Play Involving Other People

The most common reason for deliberate misbehavior is the desire to elicit the anticipated reaction; this is analogous to the fun of pressing the button on a toy in order to make it ring. Despite the involvement of other people, this type of behavior is not a form of interaction in

the true sense of the word. Instead, it should be recognized as a form of perseverative play that embroils other people.

When does this repetitive misbehavior increase? In the section on how to respond to impairments of social imagination (page 136), we saw that children usually cling to familiar patterns of behavior when they are anxious or confused or cannot find other forms of enjoyment. This principle also applies to perserverative play that involves other people.

These children actually appear to enjoy hitting people, running away, or throwing things. And in those moments, they may in fact be having fun. They do not necessarily feel confused or anxious at that specific point in time, although in many cases they do. The problem is their overall sense of security and achievement. First, we must double check how well they understand what is going on in their daily lives. Do the instructions they receive match their level of comprehension? Are they being helped to grasp in advance how an activity, or the day's schedule, is going to unfold? Are they being asked to demonstrate social skills that do not match their abilities, such as being made to interact with other children before they understand how? The principle for dealing with and preventing persistent negative behaviors is to address whatever is causing the child to cling to these behaviors.

Many parenting books advise ignoring inappropriate behaviors if the child obviously enjoys getting a response. Certainly it is important not to overreact. But what happens if we merely ignore the behavior without attempting to deal with the anxiety or confusion that is causing it? Even if the behavior does disappear, the child will most likely replace it with something else that is even more troublesome. Then there is the question of whether the behavior can, in fact, be ignored indefinitely. If you try ignoring it and eventually find that you are unable to refrain from responding, you will only have succeeded in causing the inappropriate behavior to escalate. It is true that if we are in a one-to-one situation we can manage to ignore most types of infraction. But even if a teacher at kindergarten or preschool can turn a blind eye, he or she cannot control the reactions of other children. Moreover, adults have a responsibility to protect the mental state of classmates and siblings by not allowing behavior that causes them distress or anxiety to continue unchecked. If it will be impossible to ignore a behavior in the end, then it is more realistic to nip it in the bud by, for example, removing the child to another room. Do this dispassionately and then provide the supports he or she needs to calm down (for example, leaving the child alone for a while, or inviting him or her to do a preferred activity); at the same time, assess the cause and identify appropriate measures to deal with it.

Boredom (When Things are either Too Easy or Take Too Long)

The next most likely cause of social misbehavior is that the child is bored. Children on the autism spectrum, even those without any intellectual disability, often have short attention spans. This is particularly noticeable with regard to subjects in which they have no interest. A child who bothers the kindergarten teacher during roll call every morning may be doing this because he or she is bored, in addition to not understanding. Attention span is a developmental issue and must be addressed with a program that fits the child's current level of ability; that is, the length of tasks must be planned so that they are appropriate for his or her actual attention span. At the same time, it is important to strive to make the environment less distracting and to look for tasks that are neither too easy nor too difficult and that attract the child's interest.

For example, if the child can read, the teacher can provide a copy of the class roster and have him or her check off the names of each child who answers when called. If the child gets bored with that, there must still be room for innovation. And if not—if the task truly cannot be adapted in a way that fits the child—then teachers and parents must be flexible enough to consider non-participation as an acceptable option, whether the event is the school Sports Day, a school performance, or even the graduation ceremony. We should be striving, with innovative responses and strong resolve, to prevent the child from having any unpleasant memories of life at kindergarten.

Misguided Attempts at Communication

Sometimes children may behave inappropriately because there is something they wish to communicate, but do not know how. A child may, for example, suddenly sprawl face down across his desk to indicate that he doesn't understand something, or show you his bare bottom as a way of saying, "Hello." The best response to such behavior is to teach a more suitable method of expression. When a child demonstrates this particular difficulty, chances are that the level of expression generally being expected of him or her has been too high. Although children on the autism spectrum may be very good at talking about their own interests, it is often hard for them to get at what they really want to say using words, unless they have some sort of guiding clues or prompts. I suggest considering the use of techniques such as reminders (see page 123) to help them be more successful in this area.

Frankly, however, there are surprisingly few cases where deliberate misbehavior actually disappears when a substitute is taught; most often, what seem superficially to be misguided communication attempts are actually examples of perseverative play involving other people.

I've heard that television can cause autism. Is it wrong to let our child watch TV?

Try as they may to occasionally use the television as a babysitter, parents with neurotypical toddlers and preschoolers find that they cannot leave their little ones alone for long before they are back demanding attention. It is precisely because children on the autism spectrum tend not to actively seek out their parents' attention that they can stay continuously glued to the TV. In other words, watching too much television is not a cause of ASDs, but rather it can be one of the results.

Some people claim that even if television is not a causative factor, it is still better not to let young children watch it. Indeed, living with the television on all day long may have a major and harmful impact. It may be difficult for children to tune into a parent's voice if other attractive sounds and images are always flooding the room. They may also find it harder to centre their thoughts and emotions on what they should be doing.

On the other hand, for children on the autism spectrum, who are often strong at processing information visually, learning from television or videos is fun. And there are certainly children who easily acquire skills such as hand washing and taking a bath from watching educational children's videos despite having failed to learn the steps when their parents taught them. In addition, it is important for children with ASDs to have some activity that can keep them occupied by themselves. This not only gives parents needed time for taking care of other children and getting housework done, but also gives the children themselves an opportunity to experience some independence, which will serve them well in the future.

In the end, the most important thing is to have appropriate rules governing TV-watching. For example, television can serve as a good opportunity for children to practice the skill of bringing an activity to a close.

In families where at-home interventions are not yet part of the fabric of daily life, it is not unusual for the home to be dominated by the child. At this stage, it may be impossible to work on the skill of "finishing," and television may be a major disruption to necessary daily routines. In such cases there may be no alternative but to remove the television entirely for a certain period of time.

Our child seems very interested in letters. Should we buy educational videos for studying? Or does this interest fall under the category of a "rigid interest" or "perseveration" that we should try not to encourage?

When the object of a special interest appears at first glance to be something educational (such as letters, numbers, a foreign language, etc.), it is easy for parents to believe that advanced study in this area will compensate for weakness in other areas. But it is important to remember that rigidity is rigidity, and the resulting lack of balance will not be remediated by over-encouraging a child's special interest. Your child will not become a genius just by studying that subject, nor will any of his or her problems be solved in this way. As long as you understand this, there is no need for you to remove the object of the child's interest. For young children on the high-functioning end of the autism spectrum, an interest in letters does not necessarily stop merely with letter shapes, but may also become useful at an early stage in organizing information. However, as was noted in my answer to the previous question regarding TV-viewing, interests that become overly persistent can prevent the child from dividing energy among other activities and can disrupt the daily routine.

My child is hypersensitive to sound. I'm worried about his/her reaction to the starting gun during the races at the school Sports Day. Should I try to accustom him/her to the noise in advance by repeated exposure?

We have already discussed the fact that children with autism spectrum disorders often have their own peculiar reactions to various sensory stimuli (see page 79). Hypersensitivity to sound is one very common sensory issues. Below I outline the principles for dealing with this phenomenon.

Remember that Hypersensitivity is Caused by Distortions in the way Sensory Information is Processed by the Cerebrum

People often find it hard to accept that sensory hypersensitivity is a disability, and consequently even those who are well informed about the autism spectrum tend to demand that children overcome it through sheer willpower. It must be understood that this symptom is caused by a characteristic of the brain itself. The range of tolerance in most children increases as they grow older and the brain matures.

Operate from the Premise that when a Child Says, "It Hurts!" it Really Does Hurt

Many people find the sound of a nail being scraped on glass extremely irritating, but generally they are not able to explain why they feel that way. Irritating stimuli are simply irritating. Some children on the autism spectrum find the sound of a vacuum cleaner or a specific phrase in a certain piece of music extremely uncomfortable, whereas most of us would wonder why. The way in which a sound is perceived is a product of the way in which the stimulus is processed by the cerebrum; the particular volume or tone that an individual listener actually hears cannot be gauged by others. When people claim that a sound is painful, we should believe them.

Ways of Shutting Out Intolerable Noise

If a child really can't stand a particular sound, what could be better than making that sound inaudible? Earmuffs and earplugs can be very effective in such cases. Although earmuffs were originally developed for construction sites to protect workers' hearing, there are now many products specifically designed and marketed as aids for children with hypersensitivity to sound. (A variety of earmuffs can be purchased online.) Earplugs are also convenient but I recommend trying them at home first. Many children can't use them because their ear canals are hypersensitive to touch. If your child is able to use an iPod or Walkman, you can drown out the unpleasant noise with something your child enjoys listening to. I know of one junior high school student who used a self-recorded collection of his favorite train station announcements to drown out the noise of people around him on the train while commuting to school. Earcanal headphones, if tolerated, are particularly effective in shutting out noise.

Finding ways to eliminate painful noises does more than protect children from physical distress. The fact that caregivers are willing to help them reduce such noises makes them feel that their pain is understood and that adults can be trusted. Through the accumulation of such experiences, they become aware of the value of consulting others and develop the skills to do so.

Remember that More Mental Energy Results in a Greater Capacity to Handle Unpleasant Stimuli

Even people who are not noticeably hypersensitive to sound may tremble with fear at the slightest noise when walking through a graveyard in the dead of night. The level of sensory stimuli the cerebrum can process (i.e., the range of stimuli it can handle) can change easily depending on the level of anxiety, tension, or fatigue. Increasing a child's sense of security in daily life is therefore the most effective way to ameliorate hypersensitivity.

In sensory integration (SI) therapy, children are evaluated individually and on that basis exposed to various stimuli within an enjoyable range. Although this treatment has no effect on the triad of impairments, it does seem to broaden the range of sensory information that the child is capable of managing. An SI program, however, must not be excessively taxing and should be based on sufficient evaluation. In another approach, children are repeatedly exposed to unpleasant stimuli in the belief that this will help them develop a tolerance for uncomfortable sensations; if this treatment exceeds the individual's threshold of tolerance, however, the impact will be more negative than positive. As I explain below, before considering these approaches, you need to determine whether or not the problem is important enough to require intervention in the first place.

First Ask Yourself: Does the Child Really Need the Ability to Endure this Particular Stimulus?

Children have many goals that they must work towards, and the attainment of any one of these goals is a marvellous accomplishment. Those supporting their efforts must therefore be judicious in prioritizing specific targets. Goals that warrant immediate attention are those that can actually be attained with just a little more effort and—among those—the ones that will cause the child the most difficulty if they are not achieved.

Let's return to our original example: what to do about the starting gun at Sports Day. Although the final decision requires more information about the child and the overall situation, in general the best solution would be for the school to substitute another sound for the starting signal. For the majority of children on the autism spectrum, Sports Day is already an anxiety-provoking situation filled with commotion and crowds of people moving about in ways that are difficult to anticipate. Under such conditions, it is even harder for them to deal with things that generally tend to cause them some difficulty. Moreover, the sound of a pistol shot is not something that most people will hear in any other situation. Consequently, developing an ability to tolerate this particular sound should not be made a high priority. The substitution of an electronic sound for the starting gun has, in some cases, resulted in complaints from other parents that it destroys the mood of the event. Such complaints, however, represent excellent opportunities to enlighten others about the characteristics of autism. I encourage you to enlist the cooperation of your child's teachers in spreading this kind of awareness.

My child only eats noodles and fried chicken. Should we be more insistent with him/her about the need to eat a greater variety of foods?

Several factors can cause food-related issues in children on the autism spectrum. These include unusual reactions to certain food textures or tastes (sensory issues), rejection because something is new or because it violates some personal "rule" (impairment of social imagination), and confusion about or rejection of the meal situation (the noisy, chaotic classroom, aversion to being pressured by the teacher or other children, etc.).[3] In some cases, specific foods rejected by a child are later discovered to contain substances to which the child is actually allergic.

Rather than treat all of these as a single issue, it is better to observe each child carefully, categorizing his or her aversions according to the autistic characteristics that appear to cause them, and then consider interventions. Some children, for example, will be able to eat a food that has heretofore been rejected if you simply change its appearance by serving it on the child's usual plate or in a bag from a favorite local convenience store (i.e., if you make accommodations for the child's impairment of social imagination).

---

3   In Japanese public schools, lunch is generally served in the classroom. The hot food is carted into the corridor while the children move their desks and chairs to form small groups; the children take turns throughout the year to don white aprons and serve the food. At the end of each meal, everyone helps with the clean-up.

In cases where children's impairment of social imagination causes them to refuse foods they have never even tasted, during periods of general emotional security they may be persuaded by a trusted adult to try just one bite. This, in turn, may serve as a breakthrough, making it possible for the child to continue eating this food without any further problems. In contrast, there are times when it is not advisable to try to remedy food biases that are caused by impairments of social imagination. Such times include periods of high general anxiety or specific situations that are anxiety provoking; times when the child has a new teacher and trust has not yet been fully established; or situations where the child is already thoroughly put off by the whole school lunch "scene."

It is important to assess the degree of priority that should be given to correcting food biases at a given time. Correcting them requires a great deal of effort on the part of both parent and child. Of course, increasing the range of foods a child can enjoy gives him or her more to look forward to and makes life easier. Personally, however, I do not think that food biases are actually that much of a disadvantage in adult life. Those who advocate the importance of interventions often frighten mothers of young children with stories of adults with extreme food preferences that damaged their health. It is quite possible, however, that the insistent preferences and sensory biases of these people were aggravated by prolonged inadequate support.

A major health boom is sweeping our society. Mothers are subjected to nonverbal pressure arising from the assumption that they have a responsibility to make sure their children can eat anything. They are further overwhelmed by the many health-related television programs that seem designed to arouse anxiety.

Some authorities go so far as to imply that diet is at the very root of treatment, instructing parents to almost force-feed their children.

People on the high-functioning end of the autism spectrum will probably experience the most difficulty with food biases from elementary school through junior high school. It is very important to assess whether now is the right time to deal with this issue for your child. If he or she is gaining weight appropriately, then this is not a high-priority issue. If, on the other hand, he or she is refusing food to the extent that it results in weight loss, you do have an urgent problem—but working on dietary improvements is not the answer. What you need to do in this case is to promptly reduce anxiety in your child's daily life. This means strengthening those supports required by his or her autistic characteristics.

I was told that my child's delayed speech development is due to my failure to speak to him/her enough. Should I constantly be chatting to my child?

It is inappropriate to deluge children on the autism spectrum with words that they cannot comprehend. Please refer to page 112, "Using Strengths to Encourage Language Development." It will be easier for your child to connect meaning with sound if you are brief and give clear visual information as you speak. Some children on the autism spectrum rattle off a one-sided stream of complicated jargon (see page 44). To me, they appear to be under the misconception that conversation means bombarding the other person with one incomprehensible sound after another. My experience also suggests that many children who do this have been raised by caregivers who frequently speak to them in long sentences that they cannot understand.

Language problems in children on the autism spectrum are not caused by faulty mothering. Yet criticism to the contrary may continue even after a child has been given a diagnosis. If you are being subjected to these kinds of comments, I suggest that you and your spouse spend some time considering how best to handle this. Assess how capable the person who is doing the criticizing is of understanding the truth about your child. Also consider the amount of time you spend with this person and how important, in practical terms, this relationship is to your family. Meanwhile, the best way to react to critical comments like these is to ignore them.

When my child doesn't want to answer a question I've asked, he or she begins talking about Thomas the Tank Engine. Is this a sign of selfishness?

First, look at your child's behavior from the perspective of the triad of impairments. This is clearly a qualitative impairment of communication.

Why does he or she feel the need to talk about Thomas? Qualitative impairments in communication very often occur when children are unable to process information and become confused. Thus, although this may appear to be a problem of expressive language, frequently impairments in reception or social imagination are major factors. In addition, there may also be a difficulty with the expression of such messages as "I don't understand," "Say it again," or "Please explain." Identify the cause each time and respond accordingly.

If you think your child is behaving like this on purpose, you will feel angry. But if you realize that your child may be trying for all he, or she, is worth to answer you despite being terribly confused, or trying to regain emotional equilibrium by reverting to a familiar topic, then you will feel a surge of affection. When you are able to consider what caused your child's confusion and find ways you can help, you will find that your sense of satisfaction and pride as a parent will increase.

My child says, "No jumping allowed!" while jumping up and down. Does he/she actually understand what those words means?

The parroting of previously heard words is called delayed echolalia (see page 45). In some cases, children may understand that "don't ..." and similar expressions mean they should not do something, but in many cases they are merely pairing the phrases with the situations they belong to. In either case, it's clear that no amount of scolding is going to correct this behavior, so I suggest that you change your approach immediately. For ideas on how to handle repetition of the same negative behavior, refer to the discussion of strategies for responding to impairments of social imagination (page 136).

My child is totally absorbed in solitary play. I'm worried that this will delay his development.

First, remember that children on the autism spectrum have just as much right as everyone else to have fun in their own way during their free time. If there is a problem at all, it is not that they choose to play by themselves, but rather that once they get started they do not know how to stop. It is fine to let them play alone while at the same time helping them practice the skill of stopping (see page 150). Children often need to refresh themselves by playing alone when they come home from kindergarten or day care, or during breaks.

It is actually wonderful when a child finds a way to spend time alone without feeling anxious or behaving improperly. Life is very difficult for people on the autism spectrum who are unable to spend time on their own. If solitary play is constantly interrupted by interventions, children can develop a preference for roping others in to their perseverative play sequences. These children are not content unless an adult is always present as their "playmate." The emergence of this type of behavior is often misunderstood and welcomed as an improvement in socialization (the formation of attachment behavior), but it is actually non-reciprocal and entirely rigid, and it can totally disrupt the life of the family.

The time to be concerned about solitary play is when the length or intensity of an activity increases again after a period of having been less pronounced. This may be a sign of anxiety or confusion, and it should not be addressed by direct attempts to stop the behavior. Instead, look at the content of the child's daily life and see what needs changing; refer to the section on what to do when rigidity intensifies (page 147) and provide your child with appropriate supports.

My child doesn't sleep soundly at night. What should I do?

As explained in Chapter 1 under "Symptoms Outside of the Wing Triad," children with developmental disorders tend to have trouble establishing regular sleep patterns (page 83). Some children on the autism spectrum wake at the slightest sound because they have hypersensitive hearing. As it is quite common for infants to wake up during the night, it is hard for parents to know when the time has come to seek professional help. But if your child still has difficulty sleeping through the night after the age of two, try implementing the steps described here for sleep disorders. If, despite having done this, either the parent or the child continues to suffer as a result of chronic sleep deprivation even after the child is three, I recommend that you consult a professional.

Establishing a daily rhythm, including stable sleep patterns, is a major theme during early childhood. A stable routine provides the foundation for development. If children remain sleep deprived after they have started going to kindergarten or other preschool facilities, then intervention and treatment will not be as effective as they could be. The children will be grumpy or spend the day in a daze, missing opportunities to establish stable relationships with the people around them despite having the capacity to do so. The disadvantages children suffer due to sleep impairment are by no means insignificant.

The first step is to establish a fixed routine in the period just before bedtime. In other words, use perseverative behavior in a way that leads naturally into sleep. The order could be: take a bath, change into pyjamas, brush teeth, have one book read out loud (or listen to one lullaby), dim the lights, and go to sleep. If parents strive to maintain this order, it is often possible to establish good night time habits by the age of about one and a half. But if you are just beginning and your child is already around age two or older, then I suggest facilitating the transition by using objects or picture cards to aid understanding of the entire routine and each step as it comes. Refer to the section on how to deal with impairments of social imagination (page 136). If a child has any personal "rules" (i.e., deeply ingrained habits) without which he or she cannot sleep, such as having a certain object to sleep with or leaving the nightlight on, these can be helpful as long as they do not cause any great inconvenience. They are far preferable to insistent behaviors that require the cooperation of other people, such as needing to fondle Mother's earlobe or entwining legs with her in order to sleep. Behaviors like these that involve the child's mother are very hard to correct once they have become established, but if you are in this situation try, without making your demands too harsh, to substitute something that feels similar. One common mistake is for parents to create routines that involve a father who comes home at irregular times, making it impossible to establish a consistent bedtime for the child. Considering the expectations that many men face as employees, it is often unrealistic to expect the father to help out with the daily bedtime routine. If the time your child drifts off tends to coincide with Daddy's return home, causing too much excitement for sleep, it may be better to ask your husband to come home later until your son or daughter has got into a good rhythm. It is very difficult for some fathers to comply with a request to come home early, but in most cases they will be able to regularly come home later if asked.

It is easier to establish a daily rhythm if not only the bedtime but also the daytime routine is regular. As a general rule, it is easier for all children, whether or not they have ASDs, to sleep consistently well at night if they get enough exercise during the day. But if a child is very hyperactive and you are spending so much time out of the house that it becomes a huge burden, then remember that there is no need to overdo it. Your child will still be getting sufficient exercise when you are home, and it is more important for Mom to protect herself from complete physical and mental exhaustion!

If you have tried these interventions without seeing any improvement and your child continues to have obvious difficulty sleeping even after turning three, then I think it is reasonable to consult a physician and consider trying medication. In some cases, the vicious cycle of night time insomnia resulting in long afternoon naps or falling asleep in the early evening, followed by yet another night of insomnia, can be broken with a low-dose tranquilizer taken for one to three months. In addition, medicine is often effective in treating the type of insomnia characterized by falling asleep at the regular time but waking in the middle of the night. Insomnia in early childhood almost always corrects itself once the brain physically matures or once a good bedtime routine has become well established. Therefore, medication need only be viewed as a stopgap measure to use temporarily en route to a more permanent solution. I recommend that you give full weight to the problems that can be caused by insomnia and do not hesitate to consult a physician when the situation warrants it.

Our child is going to start kindergarten soon, but is still wearing diapers even in the daytime. How do other people handle toilet training?

In addition to the usual factors involved in the toilet training of any child, there are special difficulties for those with high-functioning ASDs, including sensory issues and the tendency toward rigid insistence on certain routines and behaviors. Moreover, toilet training is a particular worry for mothers because, unlike food biases, it cannot be put off indefinitely and is not something that needs to be dealt with only at fixed times of the day.

If children do not feel uncomfortable even though they are wet, or if they appear not to feel the urge to urinate despite having a full bladder, then delayed toilet training may be related to a sensory issue. Using training pants in the expectation that your child will tell you after the fact will not be of much help if he feels no discomfort. One effective strategy is to forget about the conventional rules of toilet training and help your child to develop the habit of going to the toilet at regular intervals such as when he wakes up, before watching a DVD, before meals, and before going out. Make these intervals readily understandable to your child, saying, for example, "You can watch Thomas after going to the toilet" or "Number 1, toilet. Number 2, go for a walk" and help your child work towards the day when he will be able to go to the toilet without instruction. Through this method, you can bypass the sensory issue and solve the problem of wetting accidents by encouraging your child to adopt a healthy insistence on a rule about going to the toilet when it's time.

Consider that delayed toilet training may be related to rigid habits if your child has counterproductive behaviors such as always relieving himself or herself in a specific place other than the toilet, or always taking the time and trouble to first put on disposable diapers whenever he or she feels the urge to go. The first step is to recognize what you are dealing with. The principle for dealing with such behavior is not to try to eliminate rigidity itself, but rather to replace one entrenched habit with another that is more socially acceptable. For example, if your child always has a bowel movement in the bath, place a potty on the floor next to the tub and work on developing the habit of doing it in the potty instead. When you've reached this point, next change the location of the potty.

Or, if your child insists on putting on a disposable diaper before urinating, you could similarly work in stages by first placing the diapers on a shelf next to the toilet and having him or her change in the bathroom, then putting the diaper directly inside the potty and letting your child urinate onto it, and so on. In these and any other cases involving persistent behaviors, you must be very careful to preserve your child's sense of security when attempting to instil change. Parents often report that when they work step by step and take into account their child's particular quirks, the child one day suddenly begins to use the toilet or potty successfully. It may be in such cases that when parents begins to see the problem in its true light, they stop unwittingly putting pressure on their child or causing him or her fear.

When children on the autism spectrum have trouble with toilet training, the situation can be a major ordeal. You should not feel that you have failed if you decide it best to enlist the help of experts— that is, your child's teachers—by putting your child in kindergarten, day care, or an early childhood therapy centre while still in diapers. If you come across a kindergarten that claims to be open to children with autism, yet expects them, without exception, to be toilet trained by the time they enter, then you should question whether those teachers truly know much about the autism spectrum at all.

Chapter 3
The Way Forward

I. Find Someone you can Consult

The support system for children who have qualitative problems with their mental development despite having unimpaired intelligence is still far from adequate. In many areas, public services for the preschool period are virtually non-existent. No matter where you live, however, I still recommend that you seek someone to consult, preferably an expert. Make an effort to cultivate experts in your geographical area by helping them to understand your concerns.

Public Health and Welfare Centres

Where can you find experts? There are public health centres throughout Japan with staff who can provide support for your child.

Without a doubt, public health workers in Japan have more experience than any other category of professional at assessing the mental development of eighteen-month-old children. Depending on the location, however, their degree of expertise varies widely. The foremost cause of this discrepancy is not lack of ability on the part of individual health workers, but rather lack of an adequate system. When we take a close look at the case histories of children and others with Asperger's Syndrome, we find that often concerns were flagged at eighteen months at the routine public health screening, but that delayed speech and hyperactivity began to improve thereafter, so that problems were masked and not detected again later at the screening for three-year-olds. Without a system that educates health workers about the possible prognoses of the preschoolers they see—that is, what sort of elementary school student or adult these children may become given their current characteristics—the potentially valuable clinical experience of these professionals can become the basis for erroneous assessments such as the following, which is often heard: "Oh, there are lots of children like this. You're just an overanxious mother."

Even so, I still recommend that you go first to the public health centre. It is helpful to be as concrete as possible. For example, you could hand them a book like this one and say, "I'm concerned because my child resembles the description written here." If your child is already attending kindergarten or day care, it may also help health workers to understand if they observe your child in that setting. Some public health centres offer such services as mother-and-child play classes and child development examinations conducted by clinical psychologists (including, of course, some for eighteen-month-olds). They may also make referrals to speech and language classes, preschools for children with special needs, public therapy centres, and medical facilities such as clinics and hospitals.

A health worker with high expertise can offer constructive advice concerning how to foster mental development and self-care skills. The public health workers at the Yokohama City Welfare and Health Centre, for example, visit day care facilities and kindergartens to give advice from a professional medical perspective and also play a support role in local training circles.[1] Some parents have

---

1   Local training circles (*chiiki kunrenkai*) are parent-run groups for children who are showing unbalanced development. The activities of these groups and the way in which they are organized vary from one location to another. Some groups, for example, aim to give children an opportunity to interact with adults other than family members and to give parents the opportunity to share information and learn together. Some groups have trained volunteers who look after the children at a ratio of one adult for every one or two children, offering special classes or other programs to parents while their children are thus engaged. In the case of Yokohama City, the public health centres in some districts support these circles from the time they are first started and provide backup in cooperation with public therapy centres. Parents are responsible for managing the local training circles using grants from the Yokohama City government and money collected in the form of membership fees.

told me that they have been deeply hurt as a result of insensitive comments made by health workers at their children's public health screenings. This indicates a need to improve those health workers' skills. They certainly cannot perform their duties adequately if they discourage parents from consulting them. Even if you have had such an unfortunate experience when using the public health centre, however, I would still encourage you to go back just once more. I suggest that you clearly explain what happened on your previous visit and why it was a painful experience for you. It would be a shame to pass up any useful services that are available to your child through these tax-funded and readily accessible facilities. You can decide after a second meeting whether or not it is worth continuing to consult them.

Medical Facilities

Services offered by medical facilities for children on the autism spectrum can include, on the one hand, diagnosis (both medical diagnosis to rule out any underlying diseases and psychiatric examination and assessment) and, on the other hand, treatment (whether in the narrow sense of drug therapy or in the broader senses of educational interventions and the provision of information). Medical professionals can provide information not only to parents and other adults helping the children they examine, but also to the children themselves if they are high functioning. Ideally, these services should be provided as a package, but I do not think that there is any one medical agency in Japan that provides all of these services to all of its users. The reality is that parents must skillfully use and combine various services.

At What Age is Diagnosis Possible?

Of the various functions of medical facilities, let's take a look at diagnosis. Except in cases where it is caused by brain injuries, for example, due to encephalitis immediately after birth, the behaviors characteristic of the autism spectrum do not appear in infancy, although the condition is thought to exist from birth. In most cases the full range of symptoms needed to make a reliable diagnosis is not fully present until the age of two and a half or three, and usually it is around the age of three that it becomes possible to make a definitive diagnosis. Does this mean that there is no point in seeking a diagnosis before the age of three (or even two and a half)? The answer is no. If you recognize the triad of impairments in your child, then your parenting will be more effective if you factor this premise into your childrearing model. Basing your approach on the autistic characteristics described in this book, for example, should be helpful in promoting your child's development. The state of child psychiatry is such that, theoretically, a diagnosis should be possible at any age; in practice it is certainly realistic to make one at the age of one and a half.

Another major issue is where to get a medical diagnosis that will satisfy you. Places you can go for a diagnosis include hospitals and clinics (outpatient wards of child psychology or developmental pediatrics departments), as well as the consultation departments of day service centres for children with disabilities (public therapy centres). The guidance offices of some psychiatric and educational universities also provide an expert opinion from a psychologist. For information about what's available in your area, ask the person in charge at the public health centre or a local parents' group.

Before and After Getting an Assessment

Every medical facility has a limited amount of time to spend on individual examinations.[2] If you are concerned that your child may be on the autism spectrum, I recommend that you write down in outline form why you think so and give this outline to the doctor or other clinician who will be assessing your child. It is important that you make your points both as brief and as specific as possible. Otherwise your memo may be ignored, and your efforts will have been wasted. I suggest limiting yourself to a single sheet of A4 paper containing a maximum of about four hundred words; chances are that any more than this will prove counterproductive. If possible, give specific examples organized under headings for the triad of impairments or by type of sensory issue. For example, rather than merely writing "lacks socialization," you can help the doctor to better grasp your child's condition and offer concrete advice if you add two or three specific examples, such as, "At the kindergarten Sports Day, he was the only child who left the line and played in the sandbox," or "He keeps trying to eat snacks at the supermarket before I've paid for them." It may be helpful to use some of the subtitles from Chapter 1 or Appendix 2. If you find it difficult to organize your thoughts this way, then try making a list describing your family's current situation in order of what is causing the most trouble in your daily lives. If the clinic (or office) you will be using has a system wherein you are asked to send in a pre-examination intake questionnaire, then include your memo with this form. If not, submit it to the receptionist when you arrive for your first visit,

---

2   In Japan, an initial diagnosis covered by national health insurance is estimated to take about thirty minutes. For diagnoses that are paid for by the client, each medical facility determines the amount to be charged for specific lengths of time.

just as you would a letter of referral from another doctor. Although it would be ideal if you and your spouse could make this first visit together, if this is impossible at least try to prepare the memo together. This will be an excellent opportunity for the two of you to exchange opinions and organize your thoughts.

After the first consultation is over, you may feel exhausted both emotionally and physically, but try nevertheless to review what was said while it is still fresh in your minds. The first step is to jot down an outline of the doctor's assessment and any advice he or she gave you. If what you remember differs from what your spouse remembers, check with the doctor during your next visit. Share your reactions concerning each comment the doctor made as well as the overall assessment. Rather than trying to form a unified opinion, you and your spouse should be striving through this process to listen openly to each other's opinions and to organize your thoughts as individuals. If you have any doubts about the doctor's assessment, use the next visit as an opportunity to convey your own opinion and to ask any questions. Of course, it may also be beneficial to seek a second opinion, but it is best to do this after you have gone through the process of reviewing the first doctor's assessment and querying any doubtful points. If you seek a second opinion on the basis of doubts that are still vague, then the only thing you, your spouse, and your child might gain from the effort is exhaustion and frustration.

Kindergarten and Day Care

By about the age of four, most children on the high-functioning end of the autism spectrum will be attending kindergarten or day care. If the teachers are discerning, then your child will get good support, and you will gain someone to consult with. Be aware that the difficulties your child most needs to work on will usually not be readily apparent in a one-to-one teaching session or when he or she is interacting only with adults. Also remember the importance of weaving interventions into your child's everyday life. Bearing these two points in mind, make a priority of trying to ensure that the child has sufficient supports in place so that he or she can function reasonably well at kindergarten, even if these supports do not include any kind of special therapy class. Here, the key is having teachers who understand your child's characteristics.

What kind of help you can expect from the kindergarten or day care centre will depend not only on the quality of the individual teachers but also on the system. Some local governments will provide a subsidy to the kindergarten even for high-functioning children with ASDs as long as the parent applies for one. Some will also ensure an increase in the number of staff. Other local governments, on the other hand, do not have any support system, and the regular staff must manage as best they can. Some municipalities hold regular seminars concerning the autism spectrum that kindergarten and day care staff can attend free of charge. Some kindergartens and day care centres have a culture that welcomes on-site assessments by outside professionals, while others do not. In reality, however, most cities and towns do not offer any kind of on-site assessments or supervision, such as visits from therapy centre counsellors.

Because knowledge about high-functioning autism spectrum disorders is not yet widespread in Japan, your child's teachers will quite likely have trouble understanding his or her characteristics and behavior. I encourage you to help cultivate them as supporters and in doing so contribute to greater societal awareness. I am confident that you can motivate these experts, who have specifically chosen to work with children. After all, you have already done your homework and know what helps your child feel secure and what leaves him or her anxious and confused. You fully understand that your son or daughter's classmates all have the right to benefit from their experience at school and deserve to have this right protected (i.e., that they are there for the sake of their own development, not your child's). I am sure that you will find ample common ground between the teachers' desire to help your child function securely and your own wishes. It is my earnest hope that through this type of cooperative effort, your child's teachers will become a source of support for you as well. The best place to begin is by making sure they have accurate information about your child.

Other Places to Seek Guidance

In addition to the places mentioned above, there are also support centres for people with developmental disabilities, day care centres for children with disabilities, and various public and private therapy centres. In some areas, the local government's childrearing guidance centre is in charge of providing advice on the autism spectrum. The type of facilities and conditions vary from one area to another, and even two identically named facilities in different locations might not offer the same array of services. To find out what is available in your area, I suggest you contact either your local government or the nearest local chapter of Autism Society Japan. The type of guidance and information provided by local governments also varies. If you have already begun consulting the public health centre, you can start by asking for information there.

Once your child has entered elementary school, the ideal is for the school to function as your consultant. While the quality of the child's teacher is important, it is also important to select an appropriate placement for your child. Not all children on the high-functioning end of the autism spectrum are the same, and the optimal choice will vary from one child to another and from one location to another. The most common school placements for children on the high-functioning end of the spectrum include: (1) enrolment in a mainstream classroom only, (2) enrolment in a mainstream classroom with special instruction for some amount of time each week in a special education pullout class (often at a different school), and (3) enrolment in a special education classroom for children with emotional disorders with occasional supervised participation in a mainstream class at the same school. From my experience, in the majority of cases scenarios two and three are most desirable for children whose difficulties are such that their parents already began seeking professional guidance during the preschool period. However, depending on the local government, there may be no pullout class designed to meet the needs of children on the autism spectrum (more easily found are pullout classes offering speech therapy for children with articulation and similar difficulties). For information about the situation in your own area, contact the school placement section of your local government.

Since 2007, the government has been introducing new measures in special needs education nationwide, and public education for high-functioning children with ASDs is undergoing reform. Consult carefully with your doctor and other experts about the type of education most suited for your child. If the recommended type of placement is not available, I encourage you to consult with your local government about the possibility of providing it.

Using Parents' Groups

The most well-known organization in Japan for the care of children on the autism spectrum is Autism Society Japan and its local chapters. In addition, there are a great variety of other parents' organizations, including the local training circles described earlier and support groups made up of parents whose children all attend therapy classes at the same facility. There are many advantages to participating in such groups. For example, you can: (1) share concerns and joys that are hard for other people to understand or relate to, (2) obtain information, and (3) be empowered to influence society. Sometimes, parents themselves provide and develop the services that their children need, such as in the case of the independently run training circles. The National Autistic Society in the UK has its own schools and assessment agency, which are world renowned for their high levels of expertise.

Perhaps you do not yet feel ready to share your concerns with others or are afraid to hear what others have to say. Some mothers want such opportunities but feel uncomfortable in groups, either because they feel out of place or because they find it exhausting trying to fit in. If you do not want to, or feel that you can't, participate in such groups, I still encourage you to join Autism Society Japan. As I have mentioned many times in this book, public services for children with ASDs are still far from adequate. The most effective means of promoting their establishment is for parents as qualified voters to gain greater influence through numbers. Even parents who for various reasons cannot participate in regular Society meetings can still exert influence simply by being members.

Another option is to exchange opinions and share information via the Internet. This can be done anonymously and at your own convenience, and a wide range of information is available. (If you are moving, it is particularly useful for learning about what will be available in your new location.) One disadvantage is the possibility of errors (e.g., misunderstandings between parents concerning the characteristics of each other's children, or an email accidentally going to the wrong person). Another possible drawback is the learning curve: for someone who is not already computer savvy, online participation may seem to take too much time or feel like a tremendous burden. Nevertheless, it is worth trying as one among numerous ways of establishing connections with potential sources of information and support.

I recommend that you select whatever method or methods you find easiest, but that you somehow find a way to form bonds with others who face similar situations. Not only will these ties provide support to you now, they will also provide support to your children and to those children who come after yours by promoting greater awareness in society.

II. If There are Siblings

The Need for a System that Provides Supports

One subject that is difficult for parents to broach during consultations is support for siblings. The time you begin consultations for a child on the autism spectrum is also a time when siblings need special attention. But if there are no supports to help you provide them with that care, then you may be left with the intense pressure of knowing there is still another major issue you must face.

Every parent is aware of the importance of paying sufficient attention to the siblings of their special needs children, but it may be difficult to follow through on this commitment consistently if it means cutting down on the amount of time and energy you devote to the child who is on the spectrum. During the preschool period, it may seem as though your child with HFA or AS is capable of acquiring skill after skill if only he or she is taught intensively enough. Parents who have discovered the knack of teaching children with ASDs often want to devote all their time to instructing them. But the early childhood period is just as important for their siblings. Devoting time and energy to your other children should be a very high priority. In the long run, caring for their emotional needs will also greatly benefit their brother or sister who is on the autism spectrum.

The point I wish to emphasize here is that we need a system to provide siblings with the support they require. Myriad needs are still not being adequately met by public services in Japan: opportunities for parents to learn how to care for the mental health of siblings; childcare services for youngsters with ASDs so that their parents can spend time with their other children; day care facilities that provide siblings, whose daily activities are often disrupted, with a place where they can enjoy a consistent routine and a feeling of security; opportunities for siblings of children with ASDs to meet and support each other as they get older; publicly backed assisted living facilities for adults with ASDs who are not fully independent, allowing their siblings to focus on having a congenial relationship with them rather than on the need to provide logistical support for daily functioning; and, of course, action to raise public awareness and protect siblings from being hurt by society's ignorance of the autism spectrum. Although many siblings manage to find their own feet once they've grown up, none of these supports is currently publicly provided in Japan. Nor do preventative measures for siblings fall within the framework of general clinical practice. Therefore, if you have been unable to provide sufficient supports for siblings, this is not due to some lack in you as an individual. Much of the fault lies with inadequacies in the system. Keeping in mind that you are not to blame, let's take a look at ways to meet your other children's needs.

The Issues Faced by Siblings of High-Functioning Children with ASDs

Parents sometimes consult me about other children in the family once they have begun to cope with the child on the autism spectrum. Their concerns may include a sibling's reluctance to go to kindergarten or school; severe nail biting, headaches, or other symptoms; and troubled sibling relationships. Parents of individuals who were diagnosed with Asperger's Syndrome only after reaching adulthood often tell me that the adult siblings severed relations with their parents, and particularly with their fathers. Siblings may have many troubling questions: Why do my parents get mad at me but never at him when he does the same thing? Why does Mom always go out with my older brother? Why are Mom and Dad always discussing my older sister? Not every child will be able to voice these thoughts out loud. Many siblings never express their dissatisfaction and instead work hard to prove that they are a good "big sister" or "big brother," even if they are actually the younger sibling.

As a child psychiatrist, I hope that siblings will reach a point where they like their brother or sister, ASD and all, and can recognize his or her good points.

I say this first as a doctor who treats children on the autism spectrum. It is very important in life to have people who love you. Even if there is nothing concrete that they can do for you, it is extremely reassuring to know that you have blood relatives who understand your suffering and will stand by you when things go wrong. In fact, many adults with Asperger's Syndrome say about their younger siblings, "He went through a hard time with my dad, too," or "She understands what I've been through." Their sibling relationships are a mental and emotional support.

I say this also as a doctor who has met many siblings of children on the autism spectrum. We do not get to choose our brothers or sisters, and the ability to accept and affirm them, undoubtedly after much water has passed under the bridge, is an affirmation of our own life and our own existence. I believe that this takes a long time. Even children who at an early age appear to accept everything about their brother or sister and act accordingly (and maybe even particularly those children) may come to a point in or after adolescence where they once again question the meaning of their lives. Siblings always have the choice of cutting off ties with their brother or sister. It is only natural that the effort of rejecting this option and instead accepting a brother or sister's autism spectrum characteristics should require just as much time, if not more, than is required for the parents to make peace with their child's condition or the individual himself or herself to make peace with having a disorder.

How can we help siblings affirm their own lives when they reach adulthood and continue to like a sister or brother who is on the autism spectrum? While conceding that no one knows the answer, I have a few suggestions to make from my perspective as a doctor.

Suggestions for Raising Siblings

During checkups, mothers frequently tell me about the child's siblings—be it an older sister who takes good care of her little brother or a younger brother who is so patient and never causes trouble. I listen with admiration for the siblings' generous actions and with some anxiety concerning their selfless devotion. I am sure the parents who tell me these stories share these emotions.

Of course, we should never assume that all sibling devotion is a tragic attempt to gain parental love, or over-adaptation that will lead to future mental breakdown. Siblings of children on the autism spectrum experience things that other children do not, and through this they gain knowledge and skills that other children cannot have. We should be proud of them for this achievement and make sure to praise them appropriately. Their efforts are equivalent to those of Olympic class athletes, and their achievements should be appreciated by both their parents and by experts rather than viewed as an omen of bad things to come.

At the same time, however, we must also take these children's needs into consideration. Top athletes work their bodies much harder than anyone else to keep themselves in peak condition. They need regular and effective massage to maintain their health. And there may be times when they are advised to play a different position or switch to a different sport. The same is true for siblings of children on the autism spectrum. What type of "sports massage" can adults provide to help these siblings maintain their mental health? Below I share several points from my daily medical practice that I feel are essential.

All children are different, even if they are siblings, and the siblings of children on the autism spectrum face different issues depending on the way the condition is manifested in their brother or sister. I hope that you will use my ideas as a springboard for developing your own approach, making adjustments to fit your situation.

Show Siblings that they can Count on You

Offer your child or children who do not have ASDs concrete strategies for protecting their rights. Make sure they know this is a high priority for you. Vague slogans such as "You don't have to put up with this all the time" are not enough. Siblings need specific supports, such as a clearly designated place where they can go to feel safe when their brother or sister is having a tantrum or meltdown; a drawer with a lock that the child who is on the autism spectrum cannot open; and so on. Such supports not only have practical utility, but they are also extremely important demonstrations that the parents are serious about protecting siblings' rights. Reassure them with the message that "If this method doesn't work, we'll work together to find a better way." Help your child who has an ASD learn to enjoy spending time alone in acceptable ways, using his or her special interests and enthusiasm for repetitive play. Establish a space, however small, where a sibling can spend time alone. Done early, these measures will prove especially valuable when the children are slightly older, from about third grade on.

Instil Siblings with a Sense of Pride in their Special Role

Model concrete techniques that siblings can use for interacting successfully with a brother or sister who is on the autism spectrum. They can learn to enjoy exercising these skills and feel a sense of accomplishment in being able to use them. This approach is not intended to make siblings into "little parents." Rather, it is intended to make them feel happy and proud of having knowledge and skills that other children have not yet acquired. Look forward to the day when the whole family, including the child on the autism spectrum, can speak proudly together of knowing something that others do not.

Make Regular Times when Siblings can have their Parents to Themselves

When you have a young child who is on the autism spectrum, your schedule will be filled with his or her needs, and you will be emotionally and physically exhausted. This is precisely the stage, however, when you should also make a priority of setting time aside for this child's sibling: block off half a day, once every month or two months. It will not do to announce to that child, for example, "I'm going to play with you for the next hour" while at home, unless someone else is available to look after the sibling on the autism spectrum while you do so. He or she will be unable to relax, knowing that this promise could be broken any minute. After all, you simply cannot continue reading a story to one child if the other begins pouring water all over the kitchen or decides to cut his own hair. I highly recommend that you and the sibling plan on having your time together out of the house. Don't cancel an outing just because the child on the autism spectrum comes down with a fever. (And if this happens, don't make the sibling feel that you are doing him or her a favor by not staying home with the sick child. Maintain your enthusiasm, saying, for example, "I've really been looking forward to this; let's go!") At the end of your time together, make a date for the next outing.

In some households, the mother is in charge of the child on the autism spectrum, while the father is in charge of the other children. From experience, however, I believe that during early childhood the other children also need a chance to spend time alone with their mother. On those days, let Dad take care of the child who is on the autism spectrum. If the child with special needs goes to kindergarten or elementary school, you could also use a weekday morning. There is a special sweetness to going somewhere with Mom when everyone else is at school or kindergarten.

Make Opportunities for them to Meet their Counterparts in Other Families

It is very important to provide siblings of children on the autism spectrum with opportunities to interact with their counterparts in other families. I realized the effectiveness of peer counselling during small group sessions for children with ASDs organized by the Yokohama Psycho-Developmental Clinic as part of its efforts in the field of psycho-medical education. The clinic hosts study meetings and follow-up classes, where high-functioning junior and senior high school students who have been informed that they have ASDs can enjoy learning together. Even when they are meeting for the first time, they appear very relaxed and animated and seem to share their own special ambience. (Please note that the group and the setting must be carefully structured.) Through these groups, these children gain a sense of ownership of the knowledge given to them concerning their diagnoses during individual consultations. By sharing interests and thought patterns, they recognize the advantages of their characteristics and experience. They gain renewed confidence that they can indeed develop their skills. By recognizing their differences, they learn that each one of them is unique, despite sharing the same medical condition.

I learned that the same type of group activity was being offered to siblings through a workshop I attended that was held by Dr. Donald Meyer. Meyer is the founder of Sibshops, a workshop program where siblings of children with disabilities meet and support one another. The program focuses on participants having fun together and provides a place where they can step out of the role of someone's sister or brother and enjoy a program designed especially for them. They can also share their special experiences and the wisdom gained from them. Children enrolled in the Sibshop program generally range from eight to thirteen years old, and the movement is gradually spreading in Japan. More information about activities in Japan and other countries can be found on the official website at www.siblingsupport.org.

I sincerely encourage you to adopt the four suggestions above. In addition, let me outline my recommended modi operandi for some specific parenting issues. As each household has its own way of doing things, informed among other things by the surrounding culture of your city or town, you should of course consider these ideas in the context of your own family.

★ Use public and fee-based services as much as possible. Lightening the burden of your housework or your children's chores does not mean that you are abandoning your family responsibilities. Many parents find that they frequently need to take siblings along to therapy sessions or doctors' appointments for their child who has an ASD. Yet even adults can get fed up when having to deal with crowds or long waits. If it is possible to find a stable day care arrangement for these situations, this is generally preferable to taking the siblings along with you to the appointment. Although the fact that siblings gain experience and knowledge by going with you is of course a merit, it is all too likely that you will run out of emotional energy and give this child an unfair scolding sometime during the trip. If you must take Brother or Sister along on a regular basis, I suggest you first either go alone or only with this sibling to consult your doctor or therapist in advance about the best way to structure the visit so that it is a healthy, positive learning experience. (My colleagues and I call this approach "psycho-medical education.")

★ When your child who has an ASD does something annoying or harmful, you may feel frustrated and guilty for not preventing it, but be careful not to take your feelings out on your other children. Parents in this situation often feel simultaneously upset or angry with themselves as well as sorry for the sibling who was the victim of the behavior. At such times, have you ever found yourself venting your feelings by saying to the sibling on the receiving end, "Well, what do you expect?" These things happen so quickly that it is very difficult not to react with this kind of criticism. But when parents do so, they risk compounding the sibling's wounds. These children suffer not only from the behavior of their brother or sister, but also from their parent's lack of sympathy. It may be difficult, but try to hold your tongue; when you have been unable to do so, you can still at least make a heartfelt apology after everyone has calmed down.

★ When considering how your child who has an ASD will manage as an adult, you should adopt the premise that your other child or children will not live with him or her (even if a sibling offers to do so). I may be criticized for holding this view when so few public services for adults with high-functioning autism spectrum disorders are available. I think it is best for children with ASDs to continue to be liked by their brothers and sisters, and for those siblings to feel good about being related to someone on the autism spectrum. If geographic distance is necessary in order for siblings to continue liking one another, I think that it is better for them to live apart. I also believe that I and my fellow professionals should encourage them to consider it.

There are times when siblings tell me sadly, or angrily, that I am irresponsible to say such things and have no understanding of the reality. But it is precisely because I do know the reality that I believe you as a parent and I as an expert need to tell siblings that they have the option of living apart. Our position from day one must be that

ruling out this possibility is a violation of the basic rights of both children with ASDs and their siblings.

Take Note of Whether Siblings Might Also Have Special Needs

There is one more point I would like to make concerning your other children: pay close attention to their development!

If a sibling of a child on the autism spectrum starts refusing to attend school, adults often interpret this from the perspective of their family environment, assuming it is simply a temporary reversion to babyish behavior due to stress. It is true, as mentioned before, that these children are being raised in an unusual environment. But there are times when you will not be able to find appropriate supports if you seek all the causes in the home environment alone.

In the section of Chapter 1 on other medical information, I mentioned that genetics is considered to be one factor contributing to autism spectrum disorders (see page 88). In fact, in my clinical experience it is quite common to meet siblings of children on the autism spectrum who are terribly serious, who have difficulty switching gears or trying new things, or who have narrow interests. ADHD characteristics such as inattention (page 97) are also common. It is difficult to generalize about how frequently these traits are severe enough to warrant diagnostic labels in their own right, but in practical terms your best bet is to be cautious. In other words, if you know that one of your children is on the spectrum and then become aware that another child is also having difficulties and shows signs resembling the triad of impairments or ADHD, then your parenting will be most effective if you assume that this child, too, is affected by one of these disorders. You will need a firm grasp of this sibling's developmental characteristics in order to understand the nature of his or her difficulties and the degree of effort that he or she is making to cope with everyday life.

When one child clearly has the triad of impairments or ADHD, then it is much harder to notice more subtle presentations of the same characteristics in a sibling. In addition, parents often say, "I just didn't want to believe that my other child might have it, too." But if we are to provide support, what we need is the truth. If one of your other children is having difficulties, try to step back and get an objective perspective.

III. Some Final Advice

Treasure your Own Individuality

Every child is different. Throughout this book I have emphasized the importance of accurately grasping these differences and individualizing your approach. But every parent, too, is different. Are you utilizing your individuality as you raise your child?

What if I told you that all mothers love playing with children and that nothing gives them greater joy than making the things their children like, whether it be a gourmet packed lunch filled with their child's all-time favorites or a handmade school bag?[3] Or that all fathers are good at sports, teach their children to play catch, and take them cycling? I am sure the reaction of most people would be, "You can't be serious," yet I often meet parents who are extremely frustrated because they are forcing themselves, or being forced by a spouse, to fit these stereotypical images. Some are being pressured by their own mothers or fathers to be a "good" parent (which in the case of women means being good at cooking and cleaning). Finding ways to manage the daily routine when children are very young is intrinsically difficult, and perhaps for this reason people tend to measure the reality on the ground against an idealized yardstick of perfection.

Children with high-functioning ASDs have a lot on their plate. If we expect a child to tackle every issue at once just because we decide they are all crucial, then the child will collapse. We must

---

3   Home-sewn bags—for gym shoes, lunch boxes, library books, and so on—are part of Japanese education. Their creation is widely considered an ordinary part of responsible motherhood, much to the chagrin of those who find themselves not up to the task.

always be careful to keep expectations within the range of the child's mental and emotional capacity and to increase his motivation and confidence by setting goals that he can meet successfully. I think that this principle also applies to our own childrearing. We have a limited amount of time. Our energy is not boundless. We, too, need to set priorities.

The enterprise we call "housework" comprises countless vague and undefined "duties" that defy definitive listing and seem to bear down upon us relentlessly. It is very difficult to manage unless you are able to move from task to task efficiently, keeping your standards moderate. The type of person who tends to put her heart and soul into every little thing will not survive without making some kind of radical change in her modus operandi. This is all the more true if you have a child who requires extra attention. When parents consult me, I urge those who are not good at cooking to buy readymade meals during periods when life is rough. Similarly, for those who are not good at sewing, I let them in on this little secret: there are stores that sell bags identical to the ones that a mother might make at home for her children. I also encourage them to hire a house cleaner if possible. I do this because I know that the kind of mothers who take their jobs seriously enough to come to me for a consultation need a great deal of determination to make peace with the decision to take what seems like the easy way out—no matter how incredibly daunting they find the task before them. After all, I am myself a homemaker who takes her job seriously but is not good at housework.

Mothers who are not good at playing with their children tend to feel even guiltier than those who are not good at housework. Personally, however, I believe that each individual should do what

works for her. Trying to be someone you're not will only augment your frustration, and this will not make anyone in your family happy. In some cases it is just plainly more practical to use day care or some other means of help in providing care and companionship for your child. It may be that you lack the ability to improvise, or are poor at planning, or are absentminded. But then casting these characteristics in a positive light, we can also say with equal truth that you are meticulous, thrive on challenges, or are able to think fast on your feet. I have met many families that remained unaware of their own characteristics and wound up mired in troubles that could have been avoided. This seems a terrible shame, especially when all involved are truly making their very best efforts.

The message I hope you will take to heart is this: identify your own strengths and weaknesses and take pride in playing to your strengths as you raise your children. Show them by example that developing skills to compensate for one's weaknesses is a life-long endeavour, possible at any age. Speak to them about these things with the conviction of someone who works diligently to avoid troubles of her own. Tell them, for example, "I always make sure to write my appointments down on the calendar because I'm very absentminded. And I'm proud of myself. Even though I'm so forgetful, I remembered to go to the parents' meeting at school." If you have developmental weaknesses yourself, this means you have a great opportunity to show your children how pleasant and convenient it can be to find ways to work around such difficulties. That, in itself, is a parenting style uniquely yours.

Uncomfortable Words: "Accepting" Disability

In my work, I frequently hear people talk about "accepting" disability. We say, "He has accepted his disability," "She is unable to accept her disability," or "He is refusing to accept it." I myself have used such expressions, despite feeling that they are somehow inappropriate.

When parents decide to have children, they abandon certain other life choices. Although this is true to some extent for fathers, I think it is especially true for mothers because of the biological functions of carrying, bearing, and nursing. When a woman decides to have a child, she undoubtedly has some mental blueprint of what her own life as a mother will be like. The birth of a child with a disability is an unforeseen event precipitated by an outside force and necessitating a redrafting of these plans. To make matters worse, it requires this shift to happen immediately, despite the fact that this process entails nothing less than the redirection of a woman's life, something that ideally should not be done in haste.

Many years ago, the mother of a child with Kanner's Syndrome accompanied by severe intellectual impairment laughed as she told me, "I hope to wake up in the morning and find out that this is all a dream and he isn't autistic at all. I guess I still have a long way to go if I'm dreaming of things like that." At the time, I could only say to her hesitantly, "No. I think it's only natural to feel that way." Now I think I can articulate more clearly what I wish I could have said to her.

My mother died after a long illness before my younger sister and I were fully grown. Precisely because she was ill for so long, and because the struggle against her disease had become such an integral part of our family's everyday life, her death seemed very sudden. I went on to graduate from medical school and become a psychiatrist. Academic study and training alone do not a doctor make, so interns must scrape together what little time and money they have and use it to get experience on the receiving end of a variety of psychiatric therapies. When I was going through this, I was told many times to work on grieving over the loss of my mother, on the feelings I had when she died and how I had felt about the overconfident professionals who, armed with the best of intentions, had invaded the lives of my sister and me unable to fathom all the months and years of a struggle so debilitating that we could have spat blood.

For many years after she died, at least ten years I think, I often dreamed that she was still alive. I would wake up exhausted and ask myself whether I had really accepted her death. But every day I made supper, calculated the wages of the house cleaner, mediated family squabbles, went to school, studied, and enjoyed student life. I lived each day without flinching from the reality that my mother was no longer alive. And so I wondered who had the right to tell me that I had not accepted her death. Even now I sometimes dream of my mother. Each time I dream of her or remember her, I feel something new, something that I have not felt before. I come to realize things that I had not been aware of before. In that sense, my mother's death continues even now to influence me in new ways. To this day, I am still absorbing the fact of her death. If this does not qualify as acceptance, then so be it. But now I can smile and retort that I intend to savor the experience of my loss to the fullest for the rest of my life.

My experience is fundamentally different from yours: having a child on the autism spectrum is not the experience of loss. I am fully aware that it is presumptuous to talk about myself, but I cannot find any other way of communicating what I feel.

There have been many times, both when I worked at the public therapy centre and since joining a private practice, when parents have told me, "We have accepted our child's disability." I am sure that this is true. But I still feel that there is something I have to say.

I think that it should be considered OK for parents to say, with humor and without shame, that it will take them a lifetime to fully accept their child's disability—to reach a point where it fits naturally and without strangeness into the puzzle of their lives, like a piece that has always been there. Difficulties are a natural part of the process of maturing as a human being, so take your time and enjoy it.

Your child will grow and you will experience joy and hope that you could not have imagined five years before. You will learn from these feelings and from the new challenges that crop up. And each time you learn, you will revise the blueprint of your life and that of your child's life. Precisely because you see him or her grow, there will inevitably be times when you wonder, "He (or she) may be autistic now, but what about five years from now...?" Does this mean that you have not "accepted" your child's disability? I don't think so.

Of course, some people may claim that their children will be all grown up long before such questions can be resolved. And it is true that no time should be wasted in determining whether or not your child has the triad of impairments and in planning your lives accordingly. Our job is to provide medical information, including both a general prognosis and a prediction of the kinds of issues that lie ahead, and to share our assessment of the child's present state. Once this work is done, it is then possible for the clinician and the

parents to decide on concrete steps to be taken. This is where our legitimate role ends.

In Chapter 1, I discussed how a child's behavior can be viewed in two different ways—both as symptoms of a disability and as expressions of individuality—and explained that both perspectives are important. Throughout the book, I have concentrated mainly on the perspective of disability, but here I would like to emphasize the importance of enjoying your child's individuality. I do not believe that constant soul-searching about whether or not you have really accepted your child's disability is the only way to achieve your goals as a parent. It's important to remember to enjoy your child's uniqueness, the way episodes of autistic behavior can make you laugh or warm your heart, and reflect on the fact that such episodes are most likely going to be a part of your lives forever. Surely there are ways that will let you savor the experience of fitting your child's disability into your life, like a jigsaw puzzle piece that is meant to belong. You have been blessed with a child. As a parent, you have a right to enjoy that.

Afterword

People who have had a happy childhood have a strength that lasts their whole life. A time may come when they forget all the little incidents that they experienced when they were small, but the memory of being loved and the feeling of being content will remain in their hearts. A childhood like this imparts a quiet strength in retrospect. No matter what abilities your child may lack, you are capable of giving him or her a happy childhood, and this is a job that only you can do. If you are armed with the right information and skills, your work as a parent will be even more effective. I am hoping that this book will help empower you in just this way.

When I was first asked to write this book, I did not have the confidence to write it on my own and waited about half a year before answering. I also hesitated to confine the topic to "high-functioning" preschoolers, as the IQs of children on the autism spectrum are particularly volatile at this age.

There are, however, many fathers and mothers raising children on the high-functioning end of the autism spectrum who are at their wits' end. Their children are also at their wits' end. And the fact that there are so few books to introduce to them is a problem I myself faced in treating them.

There are still many places where it is difficult to seek a diagnosis from a pediatric psychiatrist. Perhaps, I thought, communicating in print what I usually tell parents at the clinic will help those who are unable to take their child for a medical consultation. I realized, too, that as a practicing physician, it would be cowardly for me to refuse to report on the present state of knowledge just because I think there are still issues that have yet to be fully understood. And so, finally, I picked up my pen to write.

It was Dr. Tokio Uchiyama, director of the Yokohama Psycho-Developmental Clinic, and Masaru Kokubo of the Project Planning Department at Chuohoki Publishing Co., Ltd., who helped me make that decision. I express my profound gratitude to both of them. I am also indebted to Dr. Hiroshi Fujioka, director of the Tsubasa Psycho-Developmental Clinic, and Naomi Izuka, speech-language-hearing therapist at the Yokohama Psycho-Developmental Clinic, for their invaluable advice concerning the manuscript. In addition, without the clinical experience gained by working at the Yokohama City North Regional Treatment Centre, the Yokohama City Aoba Social Health and Welfare Centre, and the Yokohama Psycho-Developmental Clinic, I could never have written this book. I would like to express my sincere appreciation to all of the patients and staff who have furnished me with opportunities to practice. Further, I would like to express my gratitude to the eminent child psychiatrist Dr. Lorna Wing, who has had tremendous influence on the kind of physician I have striven to become.

And finally, I would like to thank, from the bottom of my heart, my son for so generously giving his absentminded and very busy mother a passing grade and continuous support, and my husband and expert in a related field, Dr. Manabu Yoshida, director of Yoshida Clinic, for repeatedly insisting that there was a need to publish this book.

Yuko Yoshida
June 2003

Appendix 1

Overview of Technical Terminology and Diagnostic Criteria

1. Asperger's Syndrome and the Autism Spectrum: the Wing Classification

The history of autism as a clinically recognized phenomenon dates back to 1943, when American child psychiatrist Leo Kanner published a report on eleven case histories (Kanner 1943). For this reason, autism is sometimes referred to as "Kanner's Syndrome." For a long time, autism was thought to be a very rare and serious disorder.

In 1979, British child psychiatrist Lorna Wing, along with fellow researcher Judith Gould, reported findings of a study they had conducted based on observations of all children enrolled in special education classes in a designated geographical area. They found that the subjects included a number of children who had the same developmental insufficiencies as those associated with autism but did not conform to Kanner's descriptions and therefore had not been previously recognized as having features of autism. Wing was eager to draw attention to the existence of such children so that they might receive more of the supportive interventions that they needed. Central to her efforts was a paper written in 1944 by Austrian pediatrician Hans Asperger (Asperger 1944). This report described cases of children who showed a distinctive pattern of interaction with others, which he characterized as a sort of extravagance in personality and termed "autistic psychopathy." Asperger's paper was virtually unknown in the English-speaking world, having been published in German during World War II.

In a 1981 paper, Wing presented Asperger's findings, adding her own original perspective and coining the term "Asperger's Syndrome," describing the similarities between this disorder and autism (Wing 1981). She further proposed the use of the term "autistic spectrum" (in current parlance, autism spectrum) to encompass both autism and Asperger's Syndrome. Wing's aim in devising this terminology was to see that people with Asperger's Syndrome—like their counterparts with traditionally recognized autism—receive appropriate supportive interventions. She therefore directed attention to the common features of the two disorders and emphasized that distinguishing between these two types of individuals was not of great importance. Asperger's Syndrome as defined by Wing may be characterized as follows:

★ The syndrome entails autism that appears at first glance not to be autism but is accompanied by the "triad of impairments."

★ Individuals who are said to have the triad of impairments differ from those with typical autism and bear more similarity to the children described by Asperger. (For example, they give the superficial impression of being verbally fluent and yet have impaired communication, and they interact with others while lacking social reciprocity and common sense.)

★ In actual practice, many individuals who fit this clinical picture are found not to have any intellectual (cognitive) impairment; nevertheless, a diagnosis of Asperger's Syndrome is still made for individuals who fit the picture and also have intellectual impairment.

★ The boundary between autism and Asperger's Syndrome cannot be clearly drawn; there are children who have the characteristics of both disorders (i.e., they fit the profiles drawn by both Kanner and Asperger). In addition, there are children who have the triad of impairments but for whom neither Kanner's nor Asperger's description is a perfect match.

★ Determining which of the two diagnoses applies to a particular individual is a matter of what specific set of symptoms presents itself at the time of evaluation; it is entirely possible for a finding of autism to apply in childhood, but for Asperger's Syndrome to become the more appropriate label when the individual reaches adulthood.

Wing has not established a set of specific diagnostic criteria wherein a person is said to have Asperger's Syndrome if he or she exhibits, say, a certain number of the listed symptoms or characteristics. As the manifestation of the triad of impairments differs from one individual to the next, the diagnostician must always turn his or her thoughts to the triad when making an evaluation. And yet Wing has also said that the diagnostic criteria defined by Gillberg and Gillberg (1989) do not stand in contradiction to her thinking. For reference, I have included this set of criteria on the following page. But please keep in mind that these criteria may more readily fit adults and children who are in at least the third or fourth grade of elementary school rather than younger children.

The Gillberg Diagnostic Criteria for Asperger's Syndrome

1. Social impairment (extreme egocentricity; at least two of the following):
   ★ difficulties interacting with peers
   ★ indifference to peer contacts
   ★ difficulties interpreting social cues
   ★ socially and emotionally inappropriate behaviour

2. Narrow interest (at least one of the following):
   ★ exclusion of other activities
   ★ repetitive adherence
   ★ more rote than meaning

3. Compulsive need for introducing routines and interests (at least one of the following):
   ★ which affect the individual's every aspect of everyday life
   ★ which affect others

4. Speech and language peculiarities (at least three of the following):
   ★ delayed speech development
   ★ superficially perfect expressive language
   ★ formal pedantic language
   ★ odd prosody, peculiar voice characteristics
   ★ impairment of comprehension including misinterpretations of literal/implied meanings

5. Non-verbal communication problems (at least one of the following):
   ★ limited use of gestures
   ★ clumsy/gauche body language
   ★ limited facial expression
   ★ inappropriate facial expression
   ★ peculiar, stiff gaze

6. Motor clumsiness:
   ★ poor performance in neurodevelopmental testing

Source: Adapted from Gillberg, I.C. and Gillberg, C. (1989) "Asperger syndrome—some epidemiological considerations: a research note." *Journal of Child Psychology and Psychiatry* 30, 631–638, by permission of John Wiley and Sons.

2. Asperger's Syndrome (Disorder)
According to the WHO and the APA

Wing's proposed definition drew a great deal of attention. In 1994, the American Psychiatric Association added what it called Asperger's Disorder to the list of conditions defined in its Diagnostic and Statistical Manual of Mental Disorders, fourth edition (DSM-IV; APA 1994), following a similar move by the World Health Organization, which included Asperger's Syndrome in its 1990 publication of the International Statistical Classification of Diseases and Related Health Problems, tenth revision (ICD-10; WHO 1992). But these organizations established definitions for the condition that differed from Wing's, creating a situation in which the same diagnoses came to acquire multiple meanings.

As defined by the DSM-IV and the ICD-10, Asperger's Syndrome (Disorder) is similar to autism, but is clearly differentiated as a separate condition based on both the individual's developmental history and current presenting symptoms. In this context some noteworthy features of their definitions of Asperger's Syndrome (Disorder) are as follows:

★ There are impairments in socialization and intense and restricted interests, but not to the extent seen in autism.

★ Impairment of communication is not an essential criterion for diagnosis. (In other words, an individual can be diagnosed as having Asperger's Syndrome without having impaired communication.)

★ There are no marked delays in the development of cognitive ability, independence in personal care, or adaptive behavior such as the ability to stay calm. (With regard to language development, they specify that the use of single words has emerged by age two and communicative phrases by age three.)

Much of the language is in fact identical; in the case of Asperger's Disorder, the APA essentially just omits the criteria concerning communication and replaces it with criteria requiring a determination that there are no developmental delays.

3. Pervasive Developmental Disorders

The DSM-IV and ICD-10 use the term Pervasive Developmental Disorder (PDD) as a broad category encompassing autism and other similar disorders. The DSM-IV, for example, includes the following five conditions under the term PDD: Autistic Disorder, Rett's Syndrome, Childhood Disintegrative Disorder, Asperger's Disorder, and Pervasive Developmental Disorder Not Otherwise Specified (PDD-NOS); this fifth diagnosis covers cases where there is clearly some form of PDD but the individual does not fully meet the criteria for any of the other four. Wing does not consider Rett's Syndrome (also known as Rett's Disorder), which is a progressive neurological disorder seen only in girls, to be part of the autism spectrum, but with respect to the other four diagnostic labels the terms "PDD" and "autism spectrum" cover roughly the same set of individuals.

But here a very important distinction needs to be made: the term "autism spectrum" gathers together a number of conditions that are considered to exist along a continuum, while the term "PDD" subsumes a list of conditions that are considered to be discrete. Moreover, the autism spectrum is divided only into the two subcategories of autism and Asperger's Syndrome, while PDD is broken down into a larger number of conditions.

The figures on the following page illustrate the differences between the terms autism spectrum and PDD. Those who wish to know more about the relationships between the different diagnostic labels as used in the various systems of diagnosis are encouraged to read Chapter 1 of Uchiyama *et al.* (2002).[1] It is perfectly reasonable for there to be differences in the way terminology is used in the paradigm of the autism spectrum, whose sole purpose is clinical utility, and the paradigm of PDD, whose purpose is utility in medical research and the compilation of statistics. I believe that both sets of definitions can coexist, as long as one is careful to apply them as applicable to the purpose at hand.

---

1 An alternative English-language book is Tony Attwood's *The Complete Guide to Asperger's Syndrome* (2008).

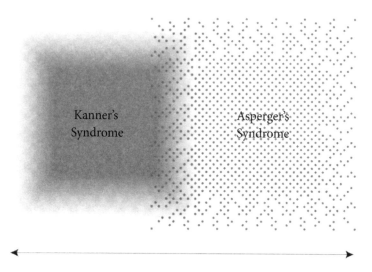

The Autism Spectrum (Wing)

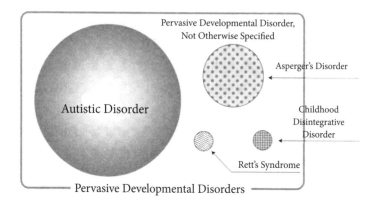

Pervasive Developmental Disorders (DSM-IV-TR)

Appendix 2

Communicating with your Child's Kindergarten or Day Care Centre

How to Use these Materials

I think it is wise to prepare some simple written materials for your child's kindergarten teachers or day care providers to help them understand your child's characteristics. As a parent, you know your child better than anyone, so crafting a letter or information sheet yourself would be ideal. But if you're a person who tends to shy away from writing, this challenge may seem daunting. If so, feel free to use the materials I have provided here,[1] which are available to download from www.jkp.com/catalogue/book/9781849053174/resources.

To ensure that your information will actually be read, be concise and use a layout that is easy to read. Avoid creating a laundry list of all your child's symptoms, and instead focus on issues that are likely to cause actual problems or misunderstandings while your child is in their care.

The information sheets on the pages that follow include space for you to add comments about your child. While it would be best if you could give some specific examples of problem behaviors that he or she has actually exhibited, don't worry if you don't feel confident about writing these out yourself. If this is the case, go back and look over the various subheadings used throughout this book and simply copy the ones that apply most to your child.

You could prepare these materials in advance and submit them when your child first enters the kindergarten or day care centre, or you could wait a month or so. In the latter case, one good approach would be to focus on examples of behavior that have actually occurred at the school or centre and explain these in terms of autism.

A final note: in the materials, I have used the word "autism," but all of the content applies equally to Asperger's Syndrome as well.

---

1   These materials are reprinted with the permission of Chuohoki Publishing Co., Ltd. from *Kōkinō jiheishō, Asuperuga shōkōgun: "Sono ko rashisa" o ikasu ko sodate*, by Yuko Yoshida.

To the Staff of _____ Kindergarten (Day Care Centre):

As (a) parent(s) of a child who has an autism spectrum disorder, I (we) would very much appreciate your understanding of the following facts about autism and of my (our) son (daughter), _____ (child's first name).

- ★ Autism is an imbalance in development (a developmental disorder) resulting from some unusual characteristics of the brain.
- ★ Autism is not a result of improper discipline or a lack of affection.
- ★ Autism involves the presence of a set of three characteristics, known as the "triad of impairments." These basic symptoms of autism are described on the following pages.

Sincerely,

_____ (your full name),

mother (and/or father) to

_____ (child's full name, age)

The First Basic Symptom of Autism: Impairment of Social Behavior or Quality of Relationships

Children with autism are not sufficiently able to comprehend how others are seeing them at a given moment, how the person they are with is feeling or reacting, or whether their own behavior is appropriate to the setting. For example:

★ Their way of interacting can easily become one-sided (lacking in reciprocity) or out of place.

★ They may be unable to experience friendships on an equal footing with children of the same age.

★ They do not have age-appropriate "common sense."

★ They may have trouble sharing the same feelings as the people they are with.

★ They tend to have trouble expressing their thoughts or feelings using eye contact or facial expressions and also comprehending thoughts or feelings expressed in this way by others.

★ They have unique ideas (their thought processes are not bound by common sense).

★ They have a great capacity for enjoying their own world.

Here are some specific illustrations that apply in _____ 's case:

. . . .

. . . .

. . . .

. . . .

. . . .

. . . .

. . . .

. . . .

. . . .

The Second Basic Symptom of Autism:
Qualitative Impairment of Communication

Children with autism can seem superficial, inconsistent, and eccentric in their exchanges with others in ways that cannot be explained by any delay in language acquisition. For example:

- ★ Their comprehension of speech may be at a lower level than their own speaking ability.

- ★ They may verbalize in socially inappropriate ways, such as echolalia (parroting others) and talking to themselves.

- ★ They often engage in delayed echolalia—that is, repeating verbatim something they've heard on an earlier occasion.

- ★ They tend to lack skill at asking for help appropriately when in trouble.

- ★ Their ability to comprehend may be reduced dramatically when they are upset.

Here are some specific illustrations that apply in _____ 's case:

. . . .

. . . .

. . . .

. . . .

. . . .

. . . .

. . . .

. . . .

. . . .

. . . .

. . . .

The Third Basic Symptom of Autism:
Impairment of Social Imagination

Children with autism have difficulty turning their attention to anything that is not right in front of their eyes, and their ability to respond flexibly as appropriate to a given situation is not sufficiently developed. For these reasons, they tend to crave sameness and to have limited interests. For example:

★ They may have difficulty switching from one mood or train of thought to another.

★ They tend to become confused or upset at unforeseen events and are unable to apply their prior experience of similar events as a guide to their behavior.

★ They may become extremely anxious in the face of situations that are new, or in which they are uncertain as to what will happen next or what the outcome will be.

★ They tend to have an easy time learning fixed patterns of behavior and to have unusually good memories.

★ They have unique ideas.

★ They have excellent concentration and a thirst for knowledge about things that interest them.

★ They have a unique style of make-believe play (repetitive patterns of behavior, one-man plays).

Here are some specific illustrations that apply in _____ 's case:

. . . .

. . . .

. . . .

. . . .

. . . .

. . . .

Other Symptoms

Children with autism often also show symptoms such as the following:

★   inattention, difficulty settling down, impulsivity

★   motor mannerisms or other unusual motor behaviors; motor clumsiness

★   unique responses to various sensory stimuli, such as sound, light, texture, pain, cold, and so on

★   strong food aversions or cravings resulting in an imbalanced diet

★   difficulty sleeping.

Here are some specific illustrations that apply in _____ 's case:

A Handy Reference to the Supports Described in This Book

☐ Make sure you have a firm grasp of your child's actual communication ability (page 110)

In the vast majority of cases, it is all too easy to overestimate the true communicative ability of a child with autism. They often have the ability to use clues from their surroundings or to rely on memory as guides to behavior, and these abilities tend to be mistaken for genuine comprehension. Moreover, they tend to use memorized patterns of conversation, which can give the impression that their power of expression is stronger than it really is.

☐ Keep your speech concise and convey meaning visually as well as verbally (page 112)

Most children with autism have an easier time understanding information that is presented visually. For example, instead of just saying, "It's time to go home," it is better for you or a teacher to simultaneously show your child his or her hat, a photograph of the kindergarten bus, or some other piece of visual information suited to his or her level of development. This will not only make comprehension more certain, but will also help your child to focus his or her attention. Another advantage of visual information is permanence: a schedule of activities posted on the wall or a bulletin board will give your child the opportunity to confirm what's coming up as often as necessary, anytime he or she begins to feel anxious; this will help him or her to accept adults' expectations.

☐ Boost your child's confidence by looking for ways to ensure that he or she can truly understand the teacher's instructions (page 115)

It is best to avoid situations where your child must resort to imitating classmates and following along one step behind because he or she cannot understand instructions given by the teacher to the class as a whole. Do not make the mistake of thinking that a minimum of instruction is adequate as long as your child is able to do what's expected. It is very important that your child be able to respond to instructions independently based on firsthand comprehension. This is the key to confidence.

❐ Prepare cards saying "Please explain" and "I need a break" to keep in a place where your child can see them (page 122)

Surprisingly few children with autism are able to convey verbally that they need help understanding or that they need to rest. Instead, they will often behave inappropriately, for example, getting up and wandering around aimlessly, throwing tantrums, parroting others' speech, or launching into a monologue on a subject that happens to interest them. It is very important that they be able to ask for help explicitly when they need it.

If your child can read, prepare cards with messages such as "Please explain" or "I need a break," have them kept in a place where your child can see them, and help him or her practice using them when in distress. Being able to see the cards will help your child remember that there are ways to ask for help and to let people know when he or she is having a problem. At the same time, they will also remind your child of specifically what to say in these situations. Some children will need to practice handing the appropriate card to the adult in charge, while others will be able to actually say the needed words as long as the card is there as a reminder. Alternatively, the teacher can point to a card and encourage the child to say the words.

❐ Work on gradually replacing rigid routines or inflexible rules with others that are less troublesome (pages 142, 147)

For example, if your child has a rule that says, "I must hang my schoolbag on the second hook," you can work on changing this to, "I must hang my schoolbag on the hook with the airplane sticker above it." This will avoid problems when your child moves to a new classroom the next year and is assigned a new hook, while still providing a sense of security by accommodating his or her need for sameness. The need to have things a certain way is very definitely an autistic trait, but the intensity of this need can easily increase or decrease depending on various factors, such as whether or not the child is feeling anxious or upset, or whether or not there is some pleasant motivation. So, for example, if your child enters kindergarten and then begins to cling to rules or becomes absorbed in self-stimulatory behavior to a greater degree than before, you cannot simply forbid him or her to act this way. Instead, you must take supportive steps to lessen your child's anxiety.

❏ Reap the advantages of your child's ability to derive power from transparency (page 140)

Children with autism are often able to work to their full potential when they know exactly what to do and what to expect. Similarly, they can often work twice as hard as everyone else once they have understood and agreed to the plan you are asking them to follow. These are special strengths that can be used to their advantage. The flip side is that they can quickly become anxious when they don't know what they're supposed to do and what is supposed to happen. I recommend that as a first step, you establish a regular routine that contains as few variations as possible so that your child will more easily know what to expect. Next, help your child learn to follow the schedule. You should share the schedule with your child visually, for example using cards or actual objects as prompts, rather than just verbally, so that he or she can know what the plan is just by looking and can repeatedly check for confirmation.

Once your child is able to use a visual schedule, he or she has a means of confirming when there has been an unexpected change in plans and resetting his or her thinking and mood in anticipation of the new activity or timetable. A further advantage of visual schedules is that they allow you to proactively teach your child how to be flexible in the course of everyday life.

❏ Make sure your child has time and a place to relax alone while at kindergarten (page 160)

When we observe children with autism as they participate in group activities at school, it may appear that they are doing just as they please, but in many cases the truth is that they are constantly struggling with anxiety as they grope to find their way. Moreover, because of unusual characteristics of the cerebrum, these youngsters often have the added burden of needing to cope with hypersensitivities to sound, light, texture, and other stimuli that seem perfectly benign to everyone else. It would therefore be ideal if you can ensure that your child has a place to go while at kindergarten or day care when he or she needs to calm down and regain equilibrium. Free playtime especially can be a source of distress, and your child should not be forced to interact with the other children. Instead, he or she should be allowed to spend this time in a quiet place doing some preferred activity, such as arranging toys in rows or looking at a pictorial atlas.

At-Home Interventions and Requests for Kindergarten Staff

On this page, list ways in which you are trying to help your child with his or her special needs at home, as well as anything you'd like the kindergarten staff to be aware of and steps you may wish them to take.

....

....

....

....

....

....

....

....

....

....

....

....

....

....

....

References

English Language References

American Psychiatric Association (APA) (1987) *Diagnostic and Statistical Manual of Mental Disorders, Third Edition, Revised (DSM-III-R)*. Washington DC: American Psychiatric Association.

American Psychiatric Association (APA) (1994) *Diagnostic and Statistical Manual of Mental Disorders, Fourth Edition (DSM-IV)*. Washington DC: American Psychiatric Association.

Asperger, H. (1944) "Die 'Autistichen Psychopathen' in Kindersalter." *Archiv fur Psychiatrie und Nervenkrankenheiten 117*, 76–136.

Attwood, T. (2008) *The Complete Guide to Asperger's Syndrome*. London: Jessica Kingsley Publishers.

Baird, G., Charman, T., Baron-Cohen, S., Cox, A., Swettenham, J., Wheelwright, S., and Drew, A. (2000) "A screening instrument for autism at 18 months of age: a 6-year follow-up study." *Journal of the American Academy of Child and Adolescent Psychiatry 39*, 6, 694–702.

Baird, G., Simonoff, E., Pickles, A., Chandler, S., Loucas, T., Meldrum, D., and Charman, T. (2006) "Prevalence of disorders of the autism spectrum in a population cohort of children in South Thames: the Special Needs Autism Project (SNAP)." *Lancet 368*, 9531, 210–215.

Baron-Cohen, S., Wheelwright, S., Scott, C., Bolton, P., and Goodyer, I. (1997) "Is there a link between engineering and autism?" *Autism 1*, 1, 101–109.

Gillberg, I.C. and Gillberg, C. (1989) "Asperger syndrome—some epidemiological considerations: a research note." *Journal of Child Psychology and Psychiatry 30*, 4, 631–638.

Gillberg, I.C., Winnergard, I., and Gillberg, C. (1993) "Screening methods, epidemiology and evaluation of intervention in DAMP in preschool children." *European Child and Adolescent Psychiatry 2*, 3, 121–135.

Honda, H., Shimizu, Y., Misumi, K., Niimi, M., and Ohashi, Y. (1996) "Cumulative incidence and prevalence of childhood autism in children in Japan." *British Journal of Psychiatry 169*, 2, 228–235.

Hoopmann, K. (2002) *Lisa and the Lacemaker*. London: Jessica Kingsley Publishers.

Kadesjo, B., Gillberg, C., and Hagberg, B. (1999) "Brief report: autism and Asperger syndrome in seven-year-old children: a total population study." *Journal of Autism and Developmental Disorders 29*, 4, 327–331

Kanner, L. (1943) "Autistic disturbances of affective contact." *Nervous Child 2*, 217–250.

Kurita, H. (1991) "School refusal in pervasive developmental disorders." *Journal of Autism and Developmental Disorders 21*, 1, 1–15.

Landgren, M., Pettersson, R., Kjellmann, B., and Gillberg, C. (1996) "ADHD, DAMP and other neurodevelopmental/psychiatric disorders in 6-year-old children: epidemiology and co-morbidity." *Developmental Medicine and Child Neurology 38*, 10, 891–906.

Lotter, V. (1966) "Epidemiology of autistic conditions in young children: I. Prevalence." *Social Psychiatry 1*, 124–137.

National Autistic Society (2012) "What is autism?" Available at www.autism.org.uk/autism, accessed on 14 May 2012.

Schopler, E., Mesibov, G.B., and Hearsey, K. (1995) "Structured Teaching in the TEACCH System." In E. Schopler and G.B. Mesibov (eds) *Learning and Cognition in Autism*. New York: Plenum Press.

Sugiyama, T. and Abe, T. (1989) "The prevalence of autism in Nagoya, Japan: a total population study." *Journal of Autism and Developmental Disorders 19*, 1, 87–96.

Wheelright, S. and Baron-Cohen, S. (2001) "The link between autism and skills such as engineering, maths, physics, and computing: a reply to Jarrold and Routh." *Autism 5*, 2, 223–227.

Wing, L. (1981) "Asperger's syndrome: A clinical account." *Psychological Medicine 11*, 1, 115–129.

Wing, L. and Gould, J. (1979) "Severe impairments of social interaction and associated abnormalities in children: epidemiology and classification," *Journal of Autism and Developmental Disorders 9*, 1, 11–29.

Wing, L. and Shah, A. (2000) "Catatonia in autistic spectrum disorders," *British Journal of Psychiatry 176*, 357–362.

World Health Organization (WHO) (1992) *International Statistical Classification of. Diseases and Related Health Problems, Tenth Revision (ICD-10)*. Geneva: World Health Organization.

Japanese Language References

Frith, U. (1991) trans. Tomita, M. and Shimizu, Y., *Jiheisho no nazo wo tokiakasu* (Autism: Explaining the Enigma). Tokyo Shoseki Co., Ltd. (originally published in 1989).

Grandin, T. (1997) trans. Cunningham, H., *Jiheisho no saino kaihatsu—jiheisho to tensai wo tsunagu wa*. Gakken Education Publishing Co., Ltd. (original: *Thinking in Pictures and Other Reports from My Life with Autism*. New York: Doubleday, 1995).

Happé, F. (1997) trans. Ishizaka, Y. *et al.*, *Jiheisho no kokoro no sekai—ninchishinrigaku kara no apurochi* (Autism: An Introduction to Psychological Theory), Seiwa Publishers, Shoten Co., Ltd. (originally published in 1994).

Ishii, T. and Takahashi, O. (1983) "Toyotashi chosa ni okeru jiheisho no ekigaku (1)—yubyoritsu" (The Epidemiology of Autism in a Survey of Toyota City (1)—Morbidity Rate). *Japanese Journal of Child Psychiatry 24*, 311–321.

Kondo, N., Kawanishi, F., Kobayashi, M., Ariizumi, K., and Yokomori, M. (2002) "Shishunki futekiou no yobo wo mokuteki toshita boshi shien no kokoromi" (Parent-Child Support to Prevent Adolescent Maladjustment). *Shishunki seinenki seishin igaku* (Adolescent Psychiatry) *12*, 2, 109–118.

Sugiyama,T. (2001) "Kohansei hattatsushogai to hikikomori" (Pervasive Developmental Disorders and School Refusal). *Kokoro no rinsho arakaruto* (Mental Clinic A La Carte) *20*, 2, 193–197.

Tanaka, Y. (2001) "Keido hattatsu shogai no aru kodomotachi he no sokikainyu" (Early Interventions for Children with Mild Developmental Disorders). In Kondo, N. (ed.) *Hikikomori kesu no kazoku enjo—sodan/chiryo/yobo* (Family Support For School Refusal Cases: Consultation/Treatment/Prevention). Kongo Shuppan.

Uchiyama, T. (2002) *Asuperuga shokogun wo shitteimasuka—asuperuga shokougun no rikai no tameni* (Have You Heard of Asperger's Syndrome? Promoting Understanding of Asperger's Syndrome). The Japan Autism Society, Tokyo Branch.

Uchiyama, T., Mizuno, K., and Yoshida, Y. (eds) (2002) *Kokino jiheisho/asperuga shokogun nyumon—tadashii rikai to taiou no tameni* (An introduction to Asperger's syndrome and high-functioning autism—in the interest of promoting accurate understanding). Chuohoki Publishing Co., Ltd.

Wing, L. (1998) trans. Kubo, H. *et al.*, *Jihei spekutoru—Oya to senmonka no tame no gaidobukku* (The Autistic Spectrum). Tokyo Shoseki Co., Ltd. (originally published in 1996).

Wing, L. and Yoshida, Y. (2005) *Anata ga anata de aru tameni—jibun rashiku ikiru tame no asuperuga shokogun gaido* (How To Be Yourself In A World That's Different: An Apserger Syndrome Study Guide for Adolescents). Chuohoki Publishing Co., Ltd.

About the Author

Yuko Yoshida is a graduate of the Jikei University School of Medicine and has served as manager of the medical departments at the North District Child Habilitation Centre of the City of Yokohama. She is currently a practicing psychiatrist specializing in child psychiatry at the Yokohama Psycho-Developmental Clinic. This is Dr. Yoshida's first book as the sole author in Japanese. It is her second publication in English, the first being *How to Be Yourself in a World That's Different: An Asperger Syndrome Study Guide for Adolescents*. Her most recent Japanese language publication is *Jiheisho/asuperuga shokogun "jibun no koto" no oshiekata* (Teaching Kids about Their Autism or Asperger's Syndrome: A Manual for Supportive Disclosure; Gakken Education Publishing Co., Ltd., 2011). She was also a co-translator of *The Autism Spectrum: A Guide for Parents and Professionals*, by Lorna Wing (Constable Publishers, 1996), published in Japanese under the title of *Jiheisho spekutoru: Oya to senmonka no tame no gaidobukku* (Tokyo Shoseki Co., Ltd., 1998). She is also Managing Director of the Institute of Psychomedical Education for Children (iPEC): www.i-pec.jp.

About the Translators

Esther Sanders is a graduate of Vassar College with a B.A. degree in economics. She has lived and worked in Tokyo since 1987. Although primarily an English-language editor and Japanese-to-English translator, she has also worked as a tutor for international elementary school students with learning disabilities.

Cathy Hirano has lived in Japan since 1978 and graduated from the International Christian University (Tokyo, Japan) in 1983 with a B.A. degree in cultural anthropology. She has been working as a Japanese-to-English translator in various fields since she graduated.